Amtrak
An American Story

National Railroad Passenger Corporation
Washington, D.C.

National Railroad Passenger Corporation

60 Massachusetts Ave. NE
Washington, D.C. 20002
www.Amtrak.com

Published in 2011

15 14 13 12 11   1 2 3 4 5

Printed in the United States of America

ISBN: 978-0-87116-444-5

Cover photos
Front: *Coast Starlight*, Amtrak photo
Back: *Southwest Chief*, Joseph D. Rago

Prepared for publication by Kalmbach Books

Publisher's Cataloging-In-Publication Data

Amtrak : an American story / National Railroad Passenger Corporation.

  p. : ill. (some col.) ; cm.

  ISBN: 978-0-87116-444-5

  1. Amtrak--History. 2. Railroads--Passenger traffic--United States--History.
3. Railroads--United States--History. I. Amtrak.

HE2791.A563 A56 2011
385/.065/0973

— DEDICATION —

This book is dedicated to Amtrak's employees past and present,
with pride, appreciation for excellence, and hope for the future.

— CONTRIBUTING EDITORS —

Peg Tyre, Editorial Director
Suzi Andiman
Matt Donnelly
Joe McHugh
Steve Ostrowski
Ann Owens
Josh Raymond
Doug Riddell
Rob Ripperger

IS THERE ANYTHING SO ENDURING and as important to the American landscape as the train? Modern America is hardly imaginable without it, and when the railroads claim they built America, they're not exaggerating. Since the first stone of the first railroad was laid in Baltimore in 1827, trains have played every role and served every purpose in the great drama of America: they have been actors, scenery, stage and stagehand, and, on occasion, audience for the vast tableau of our national story. For much of their history, the railroads ran the passenger trains—but for the last 40 years, the passenger train has been synonymous with Amtrak.

Tom Carper

The transition from the private railroads to Amtrak was a cultural milestone. At the time, it seemed like one way or another, passenger trains were on shaky ground. If you're my age, you're old enough to remember Johnny Cash singing about the trains that had already left in "The L&N Don't Stop Here Anymore," or those that we thought were leaving for good, like the *City of New Orleans*. In those days, you couldn't miss the train in popular culture, but it seemed like it was always disappearing.

A lot of people who pick up this book won't remember the last day of pre-Amtrak passenger service, April 30, 1971. If they know about it at all, they learned about it from parents and family or from books like Harold A. Edmonson's *Journey to Amtrak*. It is preserved in yellowing clips of newspapers that discuss Nixon's reelection prospects and the war in Vietnam. Every picture is different, but they're similar in important ways: the grainy grey photos always show the crowds of people who had come down to the depot to see the same old sight one last time. They came to see the familiar colors and the names they had always known on the sides of the trains: Union Pacific, Santa Fe, Delaware & Hudson, and Norfolk & Western. What a scene it was: the steam rose from the standing coaches in the cool spring air, and the trainmen stood by the steps, waiting to hand the passengers up. People waved from the windows. Then it was time. The school band played "Auld Lang Syne," the conductor raised his hand, the engine whistled, and in many places,

the passenger train rolled out of town for the last time, with more people standing to wave good-bye than had ridden it in years.

On that day, the page turned, and to everyone's great surprise, the story went on. At first, the trains still carried the names of the railroads that had once owned them, but over time, those gave way to the name we all know, Amtrak, and to the only three colors that will ever be possible for America's Railroad—red, white, and blue.

And it proved to be a profoundly different story than anyone expected. One of the men whose story is told in this book, George Samuel, remembers the president of the Burlington Northern Railroad telling him, "I guarantee you, Amtrak will not last more than five years." If this was a conventional railroad, he might have been right. But Amtrak has never been a conventional railroad—it is America's passenger railroad, and America had decided it wanted Amtrak to survive. So as the men and women of Amtrak worked day in and day out to keep the service going, with aging coaches and elderly locomotives, people worked in buildings that were all but falling down, keeping their chins up in the face of every kind of adversity, determined to keep things together. State governors began to visit Washington determined to inquire about the prospects for passenger service in their states, and Congress took note. And Amtrak continued to run, and it began to get new equipment and fixed up stations that had grown shabby from years of use and neglect.

But that's only part of the story of how Amtrak survived. People didn't just let their representatives in Washington know: they came out to help. In some places, they took over the job of fixing up their stations themselves, climbing up ladders to fix the roof, getting a hornet's nest out of the eaves, or hanging the decorations at the holiday season. They came out to welcome passengers when Amtrak couldn't afford station agents, and they turned out en masse when budget cuts threatened to leave communities far from the highway or an airport without any service at all. In East Texas, they convinced Governor George W. Bush to approve a loan to save the *Texas Eagle* with all of the unbridled enthusiasm that Texans usually reserve for the A&M–UT game. When they had obtained the loan, they persuaded Amtrak to make the train a daily operation, volunteered to help manage ticket sales, and helped repay the loan—right on time. That train serves Texas today—and Arkansas, and Missouri, and Illinois, too. The *City of New Orleans* must have looked like a goner when Steve Goodman wrote and sang about it, but if he were alive today, the *Texas Eagle* might have moved him to revise his farewell, particularly if we could tell him that the *City* has survived and serves New Orleans, Memphis, and Chicago today.

It was an effort like the one that saved the *Texas Eagle* that got me involved with Amtrak—my hometown, Macomb, Ill., was slated to lose its train service. We weren't on the interstate, and we didn't have an airport, so the train was very important. I was the mayor at the time, and when I realized how serious this loss would be, I joined the coalition that state and local officials, labor leaders, and tourism and trade organizations had put together to save the Illinois trains and the Chicago-Milwaukee *Hiawatha*. The train was one of those concerns that brought everyone out—you could see men in suits sitting next to women in jeans at the meetings. Riding the trains and working with the coalition, I realized what a democratic mode of transportation Amtrak was, and how comfortable and pleasant it could be—not just for the people in first class but for everyone. Amtrak is a unique institution, and when I go down to the station to catch the *Illinois Zephyr* on its way through Macomb, I'm grateful to all of the people who worked so hard to preserve it.

Like those stories, the story this book tells is about Amtrak and America. This is a book about trains, but it's not simply a train book. It's a book about what Amtrak is and how it has fit itself into the American scene over the last four decades. To those who are new to the subject, there will be some surprises, perhaps the biggest one being that this isn't just a story about trains leaving—it's about trains arriving. If we say that the story of Amtrak's first four decades is preserving the passenger train, we're only telling about half of the story—because in a lot of places, Amtrak has also brought the train back to town.

All of this is a tribute not just to the astonishing staying power of the train but to the American people. It tells you something about what they really want, and the ends they will go to get it. Between 1974 and 2000, Amtrak carried between 18 and 22 million riders a year. Then, in 2000, ridership began to take off. It grew steadily, not rapidly in any one place, but in tremendous bursts when a new train was put on or service was improved, followed by gentle but steady growth. Ridership hit 28 million in 2008 and just topped that number in 2010. Over the last four decades, Amtrak has changed, improved, and modernized our trains to attract riders, but for all that's changed, the romance of the train, the comfort of the journey, and the scenery passing the window are still the same. This book is a view of those four decades—a view of Amtrak but also a view of America and Amtrak's place in America. You can look out over your coffee cup at sunrise on Long Island Sound or watch the Rhode Island woods zip by at 150 mph; you can stand in the lounge car and look ahead at the long silver expanse of your train as the *California Zephyr* snakes around a hairpin curve on its way up the Front Range.

It's also a preview of the future. Amtrak has plans for even more improvements: for a 220 mph high-speed system in the Northeast and for continued programs of improvement on passenger routes across the country. America needs rail because America needs transportation solutions that will help us support its needs. We need solutions that are energy-efficient and clean, and we must be able to bring them into increasingly dense urban areas—because that's where people are moving. Nothing does this as well as rail, and I am very confident that Amtrak has a future that's as rich as its history. We've been doing this for 40 years, and I hope as you leaf through these pages, you'll see the same common threads that I see in the stories of our employees and our leaders—pride in the past, competence in the present, and hope for the future.

Tom Carper was nominated by President George W. Bush as a director of the Amtrak Board in May 2007 and was confirmed by the U.S. Senate in March 2008. In January 2009, he was elected chairman of the board. Tom was elected to three terms as mayor of Macomb, Ill., and served from 1991 to 2003. He is now retired.

AMTRAK IS AN AMERICAN STORY. On the occasion of our 40th year of providing rail passenger service in the United States, this book is a gift back to the country we are so proud to serve. There is no easy way to capture everything Amtrak has meant to the institution of railroading or the transportation it has provided over the years to the millions of passengers in one slim volume. So we have decided to let our employees, both past and present, tell the story—our story—and to create for you in each of the chapters a sense of the challenges and opportunities each decade provided. We also tell our story through pictures. The images span 40 years and capture the heritage and history of Amtrak. We hope, too, that this story will shine a bright light on the tremendous opportunities and importance of rail passenger service in the years to come.

Joe McHugh

It is hard to imagine any company in this day and age celebrating 40 years of service, especially one whose mission is the transportation of people. The revolution in technology, the instantaneous ways we communicate, the incessant hunger for new style and fads has caused so many icons of American business to fall by the wayside. It is even difficult now to remember what was happening in America in the late 1960s. But even then, fundamental changes were occurring, particularly so in the railroad business. The development of the interstates and the introduction of the passenger jet made the economics of passenger trains a drag on America's railroads. Through the 1960s, one by one, the railroads began to shed their passenger service. It was a sorrowful experience. These once glittering streamliners, which carried the names of Greek gods or conjured images of speed and progress, were parked in rail yards far away from the cities and towns they once served. The once thriving stations with their bustling crowds and sun-dappled floors were bowing in disrepair—dingy and deserted buildings from a different time. Left behind were so many of the small communities that looked for their trains' daily passage and heralded their arrival.

It was more than just trains that were lost. The railroad industry like so much of the manufacturing sector of the United States gave rise to, and strengthened, a middle class that provided stability and opportunity for generations of Americans. For many people who lived in towns with the great railroad shops like Altoona, Pa., Beech Grove, Ind., Rocky Mount, N.C., Burlington, Iowa, or Sacramento, Calif., the main street led right down to the main line and the railroad provided good jobs to hundreds of thousands of people. Just as the railroad carried people to faraway places, it also provided many a clear path in achieving the American dream. There was great pride in their work. Fathers turned jobs over to their sons, and whole families lived for the railroad. During both World Wars, America's railroads provided the lifeline that supplied America's armed forces, extending their reach across and around the entire globe. But the end came quickly after WW II, and as Detroit pumped out automobiles and neighborhoods were bulldozed to create expressways, America began its love affair with cars.

It must have been painful to be a commissioner on the Interstate Commerce Commission in the late 1960s because it was there, in those historic chambers, that the death of so many passenger trains was pronounced. By the end of the 1960s, when it was clear that passenger trains were being hunted into extinction, a concept was born. The idea of creating one national rail provider was promoted by those who supported passenger trains as a way to give this noble institution one more chance to survive. Those who supported passenger train service understood its utility for people—and for downtowns, where the heartbeat of American manufacturing had grown fainter but was still beating. They also understood that, while cars were convenient, Americans wanted choices. For those who no longer saw the need for passenger trains, it would provide this venerable institution a proper end. Through 1970, in a nation torn by war and civil strife, that idea took shape and form and navigated its way through Congress. On Thursday, October 30, 1970, President Nixon signed into law the act creating Amtrak.

Public Law 91-518
91st Congress, H. R. 17849
October 30, 1970

An Act

To provide financial assistance for and establishment of a national rail passenger system, to provide for the modernization of railroad passenger equipment, to authorize the prescribing of minimum standards for railroad passenger service, to amend section 13a of the Interstate Commerce Act, and for other purposes.

Be it enacted by the Senate and House of Representatives of the United States of America in Congress assembled, That this Act may be cited as the "Rail Passenger Service Act of 1970".

Rail Passenger Service Act of 1970.

84 STAT. 1327
84 STAT. 1328

TITLE I—FINDINGS, PURPOSES, AND DEFINITIONS

SEC. 101. CONGRESSIONAL FINDINGS AND DECLARATION OF PURPOSE.

The Congress finds that modern, efficient, intercity railroad passenger service is a necessary part of a balanced transportation system; that the public convenience and necessity require the continuance and improvement of such service to provide fast and comfortable transportation between crowded urban areas and in other areas of the country; that rail passenger service can help to end the congestion on our highways and the overcrowding of airways and airports; that the traveler in America should to the maximum extent feasible have freedom to choose the mode of travel most convenient to his needs; that to achieve these goals requires the designation of a basic national rail passenger system and the establishment of a rail passenger corporation for the purpose of providing modern, efficient, intercity rail passenger service; that Federal financial assistance as well as investment capital from the private sector of the economy is needed for this purpose; and that interim emergency Federal financial assistance to certain railroads may be necessary to permit the orderly transfer of railroad passenger service to a railroad passenger corporation.

SEC. 102. DEFINITIONS.

For the purposes of this Act—

(1) "Railroad" means a common carrier by railroad, as defined in section 1(3) of part I of the Interstate Commerce Act, as amended (49 U.S.C. 1(3)) other than the corporation created by title III of this Act.

(2) "Secretary" means the Secretary of Transportation or his delegate unless the context indicates otherwise.

(3) "Commission" means the Interstate Commerce Commission.

(4) "Basic system" means the system of intercity rail passenger service designated by the Secretary under title II and section 403(a) of this Act.

(5) "Intercity rail passenger service" means all rail passenger service other than (A) commuter and other short-haul service in metropolitan and suburban areas, usually characterized by reduced fare, multiple-ride and commutation tickets, and by morning and evening peak period operations, and (B) auto-ferry service characterized by transportation of automobiles and their occupants where contracts for such service have been consummated prior to enactment of this Act.

(6) "Avoidable loss" means the avoidable costs of providing passenger service, less revenues attributable thereto, as determined by the Interstate Commerce Commission pursuant to the provisions of section 553 of title 5, United States Code.

(7) "Corporation" means the National Railroad Passenger Corporation created under title III of this Act.

41 Stat. 474;
54 Stat. 899.
Post, p. 1330.

Post, pp.1329, 1335.

80 Stat. 383.

52-068 O

The people who started Amtrak in the L'Enfant Plaza offices, where the recently established U.S. Department of Transportation was housed, were a hearty group of people who would not let passenger rail die—at least not without a fight. Through the fall of 1970 and into early 1971, they put together a plan to maintain rail service in virtually all the 48 contiguous states. While a significant amount of rail service was lost, they managed to preserve nearly one-third of the national system, including many long-distance trains. Perhaps they understood that for any rail service to survive it needed national support and the long-distance trains formed the sinew which held the rest of the system together. Amtrak's early workforce, the ones who operated the trains, manned the reservation services, staffed the offices, stocked the trains, trued the wheels, and cleared the tracks, were a patchwork from many different railroads. Over time, Amtrak developed its own workforce and trained its own employees, but in the beginning, it was a number of different cultures and methods of operating trains that were brought together in one fell swoop. In its first year of operation, Amtrak carried 16 million passengers.

In the early days, the company picked the best cars that were available and used them to start the railroad. Amtrak trains, during that period, were referred to as the "rainbow fleet," liveried in a variety of hues and colors; they were the last glimpse of the predecessor railroads. It was not uncommon to board a Santa Fe coach, sleep in a Union Pacific sleeping car, and be fed in a New York Central diner while riding over the rails of the Burlington Northern Railroad. When the gas crisis of the 1970s struck the American public hard, people turned again to trains, and it seemed for a while that the politicians who voted for the creation of Amtrak had forethought and vision. Amtrak used this time wisely and began to purchase its own equipment from the last of the great car builders, the Budd Company of Philadelphia and Pullman of Chicago. The company bought locomotives and took possession

In its first year of operation, Amtrak carried 16 million passengers.

of major overhaul facilities in Delaware and Indiana. In 1977, the company took possession of what would be the jewel of its operations, the Northeast Corridor (NEC)—the race track for the plucky *Metroliner Service*. It was a time of rebirth and a time of gaining acceptance.

But by the mid-1980s, the company knew that it had to bring high-speed rail to the United States. Too many people had travelled to Europe and stepped off high-speed trains wondering why the world's greatest industrial nation didn't have these as well. The work to bring high-speed rail to North America started in the early 1990s as Amtrak began to electrify and rebuild the north end of the Northeast Corridor. Congress approved the plan and began to fund the project. In the space of about five years, Amtrak completely rebuilt track structures—adding new rail and anchoring it with concrete ties—and set catenary poles for continuous electric service all the way to Boston. In 1996, following a busy period of procurement of locomotives and cars for conventional service, Amtrak placed an order for 20 high-speed trainsets with a consortium of builders led by Bombardier and Alstom. Both the delivery of the trainsets and completion of the infrastructure work were scheduled to occur in late 1999; this would take Amtrak into the next millennium.

The new trainsets were named *Acela* and would replace the *Metroliner Service*. The introduction of the *Acela Service*—a word that combines "acceleration" and "excellence"—was used by the company to overhaul its entire image. Amtrak's long-lived and very popular pointless arrow image was changed to a new look. The company also rolled out an entire new line of uniforms for its NEC employees, replacing the standard blue uniform with a gray one.

Despite the introduction of the *Acela* trains in the NEC and increasing ridership throughout the system, Amtrak would have one more trip to the abyss of financial crisis. Congress, just like 30 years before, would have to decide to save passenger rail or let it die. In

Gas Pains? | Take Amtrak for Relief!

2000, 2001, and 2002, Amtrak came within weeks of insolvency. Leveraging or selling its assets simply to meet payroll, the company fell deeper and deeper into debt. Politicians came to realize that an Amtrak bankruptcy would do more than simply end service on a handful of long-distance trains, it would shut down the Northeast Corridor and virtually every other passenger operation in the United States. In its 30 years, Amtrak had become an integral and integrated part of the nation's transportation system.

The company's board of directors brought in David Gunn, a veteran railroader and a no-nonsense manager who stopped the financial hemorrhaging, stabilized the organization, and reset its course. Gunn seemed to be an omnipresent force throughout the system and, within weeks of his taking over, employees around the system were wearing shirts stating "Proud to be working under the Gunn." At the end of 2002, Amtrak reported that for the first time, thanks in part to the *Acela*, it had carried more passengers between New York and Washington than all air carriers combined. In fact, after the devastation of the 9/11 attacks—and transportation providers either shut down or were reeling from the new security threat—it was the *Acela Express* that carried the entire U.S. Congress to New York City to view the destruction and thank the courageous men and women who rushed to the aid of the injured.

As the decade unfolded, Amtrak seemed to take on the image of a distance runner: sleek, efficient, motivated, and in it for the long haul. Ridership grew, routes were expanded, and more and more states began service or added more to what they had. Quietly, the company reduced its debt and became more prudent in its business decisions. Employees stopped asking senior managers "Will we make it through his year?" to instead asking for more tools and better ways to deliver customer service. And with each year that passed, more and more of the first generation of those who built Amtrak—who poured their souls into

the company, who could jury-rig just about anything that went wrong on an Amfleet coach or an old Heritage sleeper, who missed holidays and family events to work on the railroad—were retiring.

As we start our fifth decade, we do so with a tremendous sense of optimism. Trains are cool again. People love them, and more and more are riding them. We have stayed with the small communities, leapfrogged by the interstates and abandoned by air and bus carriers. We are in harmony with the land we travel through—like a trout in a cool stream—transportation that is greener and kinder to the environment. We tie together this nation, and we still see the heartstrings tugged with every arrival and departure. Fathers hoist their children up to wave at the passing streamliners, and they look at it and wonder where it has been and where it is going. There is a place in all of us that warms to this image—the beauty and grace of a fast passenger train with its lights and whistle in the night. To provide that image is a worthy endeavor. But there are other important reasons why this country needs a modern passenger system. It brings commerce to communities, it cuts our dependence on foreign oil, it is cost effective and efficient, it reduces congestion, and in a world of crowded hours, crowded runways, and crowded highways, it is a peaceful refuge.

There is so much more work to be done, plenty of challenges, and the need to constantly prove that Amtrak is a good steward and worthy benefactor of the public's investment. So on behalf of all our employees, those who worked at Amtrak and those who still do, we celebrate 40 years of serving our nation, and we thank the millions of people who have ridden our trains and who have supported our endeavor. And we thank our employees without whom this celebration would not be possible.

Joe McHugh is the vice president of Government Affairs and Corporate Communications and also serves on Amtrak's Executive Committee. He joined Amtrak in 1994.

> People love Amtrak trains and more and more are riding them.

At the end of 2002, Amtrak reported that for the first time, thanks in part to the *Acela Express*, it had carried more passengers between New York and Washington than all air carriers combined. Here, *Acela Express* 2167 heads southbound through Bristol, Pa.

As Amtrak began in 1971, it largely operated with older passenger equipment and locomotives inherited from freight railroads, but it also inherited modern equipment, such as *Metroliner* 822 which had only been in service for two years on the day Amtrak began service.

The Journey Begins

Ann Owens collection

I CAME TO AMTRAK IN THE MID-1970s after a career in the Illinois Central (IC) and Baltimore and Ohio (B&O) Railroads (the latter operated jointly with the Chesapeake and Ohio (C&O) Railway—the route today followed by Amtrak's *Cardinal*. It was a challenging moment; for a lot of the railroad industry, the 1970s were a very dark time. The freight companies could neither set prices nor abandon service on unprofitable or redundant lines, and the shift of industry to the Sun Belt meant that a lot of carriers (particularly in the Northeast) had too much track and not enough customers.

These same problems had afflicted the passenger business. Both the B&O and the IC had worked hard to lure travelers to their trains, and a lot of effort went into sustaining the passenger business in the 1950s and 1960s—and train performance was important to top executives. When I was working as a division engineer on the B&O in Ohio, I knew that if I delayed the *Capitol Limited*, I would get a call from the president of the railroad! They worked long and hard to sustain service, but as the interstate system developed in the 1960s, and the mail business vanished, we knew the privately operated passenger train was a lost cause. The formation of Amtrak came as a great relief to the freight companies—because it allowed them to focus on survival.

Paul Reistrup

But if the 1970s were a time of trial for the freight companies, they were a time of growth and expansion as the newly formed Amtrak raced against time to implement new ideas that could control costs and develop the services that would improve revenues. We always knew that Amtrak's survival was not a foregone conclusion. The Nixon administration considered it an experiment and might have let it pass if the 1973 energy crisis had not awakened people to the need for transportation alternatives. This pessimistic attitude contributed to Amtrak's growing pains when the company ordered heavy six-axle electric (E60s) and diesel locomotives (SDP40Fs) in the hope that they could eventually be resold to the freight railroads; they were plagued by derailment problems, adding to the challenges we faced in operating a company in transition.

I joined Amtrak in March 1975, replacing Roger Lewis as Amtrak's second CEO; Roger became the board chairman, and we worked closely on some major policy issues, such as the acquisition of the car and locomotive shop at Beech Grove, Ind. Shortly after I arrived at Amtrak, Congress passed the Railroad Revitalization and Regulatory Reform Act, usually known as the "4R Act." President Ford signed the law in February 1976, and it changed the history of Amtrak by deeding the Penn Central route between Boston, New York, and Washington—the Northeast Corridor—to Amtrak. This was a watershed; we were on a countdown to the biggest transition this company had ever made—from a company that simply ran and marketed trains to a fully integrated railroad.

The transition came on April 1, 1976, the day Conrail was formed. Planning for it had been going on at a feverish pace in the previous months, and on that day, Amtrak formally took over the Northeast Corridor (NEC), the connecting Keystone Line to Harrisburg, and the line from New Haven, Conn., to Springfield, Mass. At the time, the NEC was handling about 960 trains a day, 120 of which were Amtrak trains, and 660 of which were commuter trains. It was a very different operation from today's NEC, which handles almost 2,000 daily trains on the same infrastructure! Penn Central had deferred a lot of maintenance, and for the most part, maximum speed did not exceed 80 mph. The track was aging rail in 39-foot lengths, fastened with fishplates and bolts, and if you knelt next to it and squinted down the line, it looked as bumpy as it rode because the ends of the rails wore more rapidly than the center. All of the signal towers were still manned, and in many places, the switches and signals were actuated not by electricity or compressed air, but by the strong back of the tower operator. It was a 1940s-era railroad, and the air of shabbiness in the buildings and stations was unmistakable.

The process of severing a piece of railroad from the larger body of Conrail was a real challenge and required careful coordination, but by September 1976, we had taken over most of the dispatching and maintenance and about 7,600 people. We put an emergency investment of more than $6 million into track rehabilitation—and this would be followed by the massive program of investment known as the Northeast Corridor Improvement Project (NECIP), which transformed the line into a 125 mph speedway. These improvements took time, but they worked—and they probably saved high-speed passenger rail in America. By separating the corridor from the newly formed Conrail, the 4R Act relieved that company of the expense of maintaining facilities for passenger service. By giving it to Amtrak, and funding a program of improvement, Congress gave us an opportunity to show the public what we could do, increasing speeds and cutting trip times between New York, Washington, and Boston.

Roger had made a lot of progress on our chief need, equipment procurement, and by the time he left the position of board chair in December 1975, the Budd Company was turning out an Amfleet car a day. These cars, which are simple and durable, owed a lot to the basic *Metroliner* design; they are still in service today, and they are the backbone of the Amtrak fleet on the East Coast. For the western trains, we needed something a little different, and so I signed the order for the first Superliners from Pullman Standard in April 1975. This project, which had been germinating for years, has provided Amtrak with a durable and attractive high-capacity fleet that is still well suited to the needs of today's long-distance trains.

Both of these fleets were delivered with a standardized 480 volt electrical system, and they were electrically heated—but they would take time to deliver, particularly the Superliners. To address the immediate need for good equipment, we went through the existing fleet and identified the cars that would best suit our needs, and we began to rebuild them. All of the existing cars were steam heated, and we began to convert them to electric power as quickly as we could. The old steam system was always vulnerable to cold, and a major freeze-up in the Chicago yards in the winter of 1977 highlighted that vulnerability. Our newly acquired Beech Grove shop force (and the shop forces of our partner railroads) worked around the clock to convert existing cars to electric power and replace the steam boilers that the engines still carried with the equipment they needed to power trains. This required some odd stopgap solutions, and for some years, we operated cars that had been rebuilt to carry steam boilers or electric generators so that we could mate elderly electric locomotives with Amfleet cars on the NEC or new diesels with older steam-heated cars on the long-distance trains. We also ordered new engines to replace the unsuitable six-axle diesels with four-axle engines designed for Amtrak service.

We also experimented with new passenger services. In an effort to build support, we responded to both communities and congressmen who wanted to see service expanded, and we added many trains to the system in the mid-1970s. During the Carter administration, we had to make some hard choices. Some services were cut, but many of the trains instituted in the 1970s were viable and useful, and they are in service today—trains like the *Lake Shore Limited*, the *Palmetto*, and the *Colonial* (now in *Northeast Regional Service*).

I left Amtrak on May 31, 1978, and I was succeeded by Alan Boyd, who brought the company through the challenges of the late 1970s and early 1980s. It's amazing to me how Amtrak has managed to change over the years, while still maintaining its focus on its core mission—to operate passenger trains. When we started our work on the NECIP, we hoped that it would someday lead to something like *Acela*—but it's still a little staggering to see those trains and to see the graphs and charts that demonstrate the contribution they're making to transportation in America. Time has worked its wear on all the railroaders of my generation, but it was wonderful to work with all these well-meaning, fine people who were facing a huge challenge. I'm confident that if the men and women who are running Amtrak today are as dedicated and skilled as the people I once knew, they will continue to improve it, and the train will once again come into its own as America's favorite means of transportation. I am grateful, as well, for having been a part of Amtrak's early formation. They were some of the best days of my railroad career.

Paul Reistrup served as president of Amtrak from 1974 to 1978. Paul retired from CSX as vice president of Passenger Integration in 2003. He is currently an independent transportation consultant.

1970

About 400 passenger
trains are in operation
prior to Amtrak

1971

INTERCITY RAILROAD PASSENGER ROUTES
National Railroad Passenger Corporation

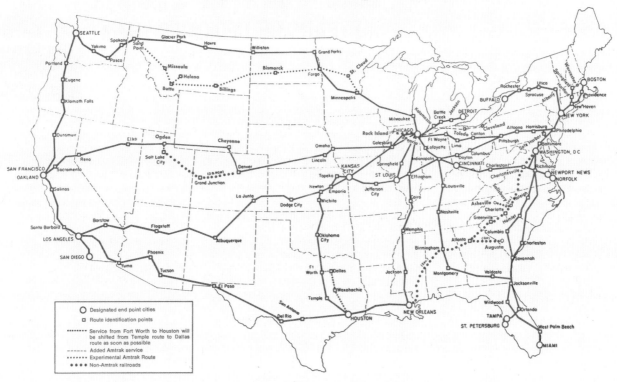

Amtrak photo

U.S. Secretary of Transportation John Volpe,
Amtrak President Roger Lewis, and Amtrak
Board of Incorporators Chairman David W.
Kendall unveil Amtrak's first route map.

Bev Balanda: Eye of the Storm

Bev Balanda knows a thing or two about Amtrak's corporate culture. The first permanent employee to be hired, she spent more than 27 years in the front office, working for every president from Paul Reistrup to Tom Downs. Looking back on it now, she says her proudest achievement was having each departing president think highly enough of her to recommend her to the next. "That was so rewarding," she says. "They felt I knew how to operate a front office and do so efficiently. I was very loyal to them, and they were very loyal to me."

At 28, newly married and fresh out of Binghamton, N.Y., she was grateful to have a job in "recession-proof Washington." After answering a newspaper ad, she was hired to be one of a handful of people assisting the incorporators who were actually setting up the Amtrak structure. She says, "I was assigned to work for two of them simply because the telephone on my desk connected to their offices!" She says that the little group was so busy setting up the new offices that they barely had time to think about the main mission of starting up a national rail passenger system.

Once everything was up and running, and she had assumed her position in the president's office, she realized that the job was going to be both hectic and eye-opening. "We had many 10- to 12-hour days. I was working on schedules and preparing material for staff members to prepare for hearings. Those endless hearings begging for money! We had to make sure that the president had all the most up-to-date information to take to the Hill."

The presidents awed her, with the scope of their knowledge and their eccentricities. When Paul Reistrup arrived, he said he was going to ride every one of the 26,000 miles that were in the system at that time. "He never bought a ticket and I could never find him because he'd hop from train to train in all directions, so we never knew where he was. He did it on a weekly basis!" Reistrup was an avid collector of railroad memorabilia, which he would proudly show off around the office. "One day he came in with a decades-old, rusted-out oilcan and said, 'Bev, look what someone gave me!' And he tipped it over my typewriter, as if to oil it. Black gritty stuff poured out all over the machine!"

Of course she wasn't just using a typewriter in those years; she was taking shorthand too, particularly from W. Graham Claytor Jr., a highly distinguished transportation executive who had been editor of the *Harvard Law Review* and President Carter's secretary of the navy. He was also a Southern gentleman in his 70s, and he brought his own emphasis to the very male culture of the railroad. He called Bev "madam," and since he hated the intercom, he would summon her by yelling the word. "I didn't mind it one bit," says Bev tranquilly. "That was his way of telling me I was the lady in charge."

Although Claytor was a little intimidating, she loved listening to him. "He would come in and sit down and something would jog his memory about the Civil War, and he'd say, 'Madam, have you ever been to Manassas?' And he'd tell you about battles for half an hour."

Inevitably, there was discrimination. Claytor had brought with him a clerical assistant, Sid Wheeler. Male secretaries were common in the rail industry because the top executives had to travel and couldn't take female secretaries on overnight trips. So when Claytor traveled, Wheeler went with him. Bev liked Wheeler well enough but wasn't happy when he exceeded her wages, even though she had put in a longer service time. Still, she did not complain. "I knew it would do absolutely no good. That was the older generation."

The reverse side of this paternalism was protectiveness. Bev remembers a story from her earliest days, when she was working for Reistrup. Her husband was out of town, her daughter was an infant, and there was a rapist at large in her neighborhood. Reistrup arranged to have an Amtrak police officer follow her home and make sure the house was safe before she went in. That happened every night until the rapist was caught.

As dedicated as she was to the men for whom she worked, Bev was even more dedicated to her job. If there was a snowstorm, or any kind of emergency, she'd get there somehow. "You did not call in to say you couldn't make it. The trains are going to run no matter what." If necessary, she'd sleep in the office to cover the phones.

Her devotion to the job meant keeping a distance from colleagues. "The front office was an extremely stressful place to work. I was the

one who had to formulate a system on how to operate a front office, what was important and not important, who could get in. I avoided personal friendships in the office because I felt it would interfere with my management—and anyway, at the end of a long day, the last thing you wanted to do was go out with the girls."

Operating on a shoestring budget was a challenge. In 1971, Amtrak had ended up with a hodgepodge of old equipment and a booking system that consisted of a group of people sitting on the phone, taking down reservations and telling you where to pick up your tickets. There was a desperate need for new equipment, uniforms, and passenger cars, and the Hill was reluctant to provide the money. Instead, as she describes it, Amtrak was endlessly required to do more with less and absorb funding cuts by RIFs (reductions in force).

During the time she worked for Alan Boyd, a very popular president who liked to wander into people's offices, introduce himself, and chat for a while, headquarters was faced with reducing its personnel by several hundred. "I found it terribly difficult to look these people in the eye when I knew that in a week or two they were going to be jobless. These were innocent people who just happened to be in the wrong place at the wrong time," Bev says. "That's why it was really important to remain neutral."

Bev admits that when she hit her 30 years, she was happy to leave the difficulties behind and spend time with her long-suffering husband. But she never forgot her mentors—notably, Alan Boyd, who's in his late 80s now and living in Seattle. "We call each other every month or two to see how we're both doing." She has good memories of all that she learned—and cherished letters of recommendation from every leader she served.

U.S. Department of Transportation releases preliminary report on routes to Congress
November 30

December 30
Congress confirms Incorporators of Amtrak

All in the Family premieres on CBS
January 12

March 22
Amtrak formally announces the routes it intends to use

Amtrak is incorporated in Washington, D.C.
March 30

May 1
Amtrak begins service

Revised timetable includes first state-supported 403(b) trains
July 12

Initially, local schedules for the National Railroad Passenger Corporation's trains were developed by the various railroads that previously operated the routes, and the nationwide schedule, including this first edition, was published by Amtrak.

Papers across the country, including the *Ludington Daily News* (in Michigan), announce Amtrak's first day of operation on May 1, 1971, although the new service is referred to as Amtrack in the headline.

Amtrak's southbound *City of New Orleans*, still in predecessor Illinois Central colors and lettering, pulls into Carbondale, Ill., on the first day of operation.

Don Crimmin

Valerie and George Samuel: Finding Careers and Life Partners

Back in the 1970s, they were two young people making their way in a new country. Amtrak brought them together—and gave them a professional home for the bulk of their adult lives.

George was born and raised in India. He had come to America in 1965 to attend college and was working as the assistant controller of Washington's Mayflower Hotel, where he saw J. Edgar Hoover arrive every day for a solitary lunch. When the company he worked for sold the hotel, he moved over to Amtrak. It was a shot in the dark, he says, but at $10,000 a year, the salary was better than his previous one.

Working for the railroad gave George an opportunity to see the country. As one of 25 people hired to audit the different railroads that were operating under the Amtrak umbrella, George traveled all over the country, including Florida in the summer and Minnesota in the winter. He used a rented car, usually a new Plymouth Fury III, to drive to the next station. One February, when George was auditing Burlington Northern's operations in Montana, it was so cold that he ended up sleeping between the mattress and the box spring.

Val came from Burma, the child of a Burmese mother and an Indian father. Val had come to America with a husband, a Peace Corps volunteer returning to New Hampshire. After several years, they moved to Washington, and Val contacted Amtrak because she had heard such good things about the company and was offered a job in 1974. She loved her first job in the Computer Services department even though the pressure was intimidating. Conscientious and shy, she toiled long hours and weekends and was reluctant to speak up. Five years in, however, a new boss noticed that she was taking on too much work, and sent her to Chicago for assertiveness training. "Slowly I applied the things I'd learned. I learned how to say no!" she says with a gentle giggle. She stayed in Computer Services for seven years and then, when her boss moved to Finance, she went with him. "I was ambitious," she says, "but I've always been in administration, which is a safer way to be ambitious."

It was years before Valerie and George would meet. They finally connected in 1986, when Val was working for the chief financial officer. George would often call one of the senior directors and, says Val, "He was the only person who would not identify himself because he expected me to recognize his voice. My first impression? I thought he was arrogant." George chimes in, "My first impression was that you were beautiful, caring, and understanding, and you had lovely long hair."

After Valerie's marriage collapsed in 1988, she used public transportation to get to work. One day when she was waiting at the bus

stop, George, who lived nearby, stopped and gave her a lift. It was to be the first of many. "He was very friendly and outgoing (opposite of me) and would sing along with the radio all the way." They married in 1997. When they committed to each other, it was a big undertaking: Val had four children between the ages of 7 and 15, and George had two older children in their 20s. "We had our two big careers while we were blending our families—and we certainly had our ups and downs!" Fortunately, Val's mother lived with them for years, helping with the children, and they managed somehow.

George has vivid memories of the earliest days, when the can-do spirit infused Amtrak employees—and making it up as they went along was the order of the day. Take the benefits structure, for example. "A supervisor put us all in a room and asked us what benefits we wanted. And that was what we got!" Much of the accounting work was done with a comptometer, an ancient, bulky machine with 80 keys. "Then we got adding machines," he says. "In 1981, we got a computer. There were six computers in one room, and you had to sign up for a time to use them."

He reminisces about his first Amtrak Christmas party. Since the company was government funded, the event was technically against the rules. Their rule-breaking party was hardly lavish: people sitting awkwardly in a small conference room being served punch and cake. George, still very new at this point, turned to the man sitting on his right and said, "Who here is Roger Lewis (Amtrak's first president)?" The man said, "He's the guy sitting on your left." (And the next day, Jack Anderson, the famously combative *Washington Post* columnist,

wrote a piece lambasting Amtrak for holding a fancy "do.")

Both cite the 1994-1996 tenure of Elizabeth Reveal, the first female chief financial officer, as a particularly creative and exciting time. Val, who was Reveal's senior executive assistant, says of her, "She empowered us, gave us authority and responsibilities. It was all first names, casual wear on Fridays—she was ahead of her time for Amtrak! Productivity increased, and everyone looked forward to working." As manager of finance, George prepared the graphics for Reveal's board meetings and says, "She had a two-inch-thick report and would say, go to page 496, paragraph 2, line 3. That's how brilliant she was!" He adds, "She gave me a confidence and a level of trust that I'd never had before."

George relished the challenges of the different jobs he held, "the activity and the changes kept me excited." Val admired all her bosses and the professionalism of the team. Despite—or perhaps because of—her deliberately low profile, Val was noticed, and awarded a President's Service and Safety Award for Sustained Excellence in 2006.

George and Val got something else too: a shared feeling of pride in the company. They still contribute to the railroad: George is a consultant for Amtrak, and Val is still contentedly in place as the chief financial officer's senior assistant. "I have a super boss," she says, "It's D.J. Stadtler, the nicest executive I've ever met. He is so wonderful, not just brilliant but kind and considerate and the reason I have postponed my retirement."

The company gave both of them careers they enjoyed—and life partners they cherish.

National advertising
campaign begins in
August

Central reservation
system begins operation
in Chicago
October 1

October 1
Walt Disney World
opens in Orlando

1972

President Nixon
inaugurates Space
Shuttle program
January 5

January 16
Consolidated tariff book is published,
providing basic fare information, and it
replaces more than 100 previous books

Phil Gosney

Train 301, the *Prairie State*, which operated between Milwaukee and St. Louis, departs from Chicago in April 1972. Mixed color schemes were a common sight on Amtrak trains in the early 1970s due to inheriting equipment previously owned by 20 different railroads virtually overnight.

Amtrak photo

Attendant Julie Byrne tends to a table in a dining car that has been updated with classic 1970s vibrant colors.

Amtrak photo

955 L'Enfant Plaza, Washington, D. C., was home of Amtrak's first corporate headquarters.

Ed Courtemanch: The Man and the Yellow Horse

You hear about a guy who's been working for Amtrak for 40 years, as long as the company has been in business—the only employee who can claim this distinction. And when you think of what he's been through—rallying officials to set up the first state-supported passenger train in the United States, not to mention being a part of the railroad industry's rise, dip, and transformation under seven presidents—you might think, "Now there's a guy who is ready to retire."

But you would not be thinking about Edgar Courtemanch. To say that Ed Courtemanch is a clear-eyed thinker who lives resolutely in this exact moment, and who sees no reason to wax nostalgic about anything at all, is to announce that Buffalo, N.Y., is near a waterfall. He's the "house cynic," he says, the guy who "gives you the tree with the bark on, not off"—the kind, he says, "who tells it like it is." He likens himself to Morris the Cat, curmudgeonly spokes-animal for 9 Lives cat food throughout the 1970s and '80s, advertised as "the world's most finicky cat." The more you talk to Ed, the more apt that comparison becomes. A bit jaded? Yes. Tenacious and durable? Definitely. Like Morris and his nine lives—and like the railroad business itself—Ed Courtemanch is, and has always been, in it for the long haul.

Like many career Amtrak employees, Ed may have simply been born with wanderlust: "planes, trains, trucks—I always loved travel," he says of early daydreams of venturing beyond his hometown of Fairfield, Conn. After graduating from Georgetown University with a degree in economics and serving in Vietnam, Ed considered working for the trucking and airline industries but came to a conclusion that befits his pragmatic disposition. "Airlines are glamorous, but people basically have to work there for free," he says,

pointing out that regional airline pilots often don't earn much more than $20,000 a year. Moreover, trucking was too solitary an occupation for his taste. The railroad industry not only paid well but also promised what was to him the most satisfying part of travel: meeting and working with people from all around the country.

But when Ed began his railroad career in 1965, working for the oldest railroad in America, the Baltimore & Ohio Railroad (B&O), the people-moving part of the industry was on its way to being phased out. Founded in 1827, the B&O in its heyday had been one of the pre-eminent American railroads, connecting the mid-Atlantic states with the Midwest. More than a century later, the majority of private railroad executives had all but abandoned passenger service for more lucrative freight operations, and many passenger trains stood rusting in the yards, waiting to be scrapped.

When Amtrak was founded in the spring of 1971, with the goal of rebuilding passenger train service in the United

States, its mission called powerfully to Ed. The 30th employee to be hired at Amtrak, Ed was interviewed by Roger Lewis, the company's first president; staff was too scant in the early days for anyone else to do the interviewing. There was also no business development staff in place, so when Ed was charged, out of the gate, with setting up Amtrak's first state-supported passenger train, the *Illinois Zephyr*, he made the arrangements, working with officials from the state of Illinois and the Burlington Northern Railroad. The grassroots network he built back then, one connection at a time, formed the chassis of today's vast network of state-supported trains.

But start probing Ed about his career's highs and lows—or ask him to reflect on great moments in Amtrak history—and the likely response will be a Morris the Cat-like sigh, followed by what he likes to call "the yellow horse" metaphor. "Working at Amtrak as long as I have is like standing next to a merry-go-round," he intones wryly. "The yellow horse always comes around again." In other words, there is rarely

anything new under the sun: if you stick around in any industry long enough, you begin to see that there are no new ideas or business models but rather old ones that surface over and over again.

That's fair enough, and maybe particularly so for Amtrak, whose fate is invariably linked to the political will of every new Congress or administration. "Only three people now in Congress were in Congress when Amtrak was created," Ed asserts, not a little exasperated. "When certain politicians or ideologues start arguing that we should privatize passenger rail service to make it profitable, there is very little institutional memory about what it was like when passenger rails were privately operated." He points out that Amtrak took over passenger train operations from more than 20 private companies that all lost millions of dollars every year operating them.

In his view, there is only one thing that has worked consistently: constancy of purpose. "In the railroad business, success is measured in years," he says, pointing out that it takes a year and a half to make a locomotive engineer alone. "You need to do the same things long enough to achieve results." Improving cost recovery, safety, and service quality are, according to Ed, the top three goals that can be achieved over time.

But don't get him started on the idea of resurrecting the romance of old style train travel. "The days of the Pullman porter are gone—too expensive and impractical," he growls. "That duck won't quack." And definitely don't get him started on airline travel. "Flying is not only impersonal, it's a serious hassle, and it's getting to be a health risk," Ed fumes. "I ran into my first x-ray machine at an airport the other day—I don't need the radiation!" Morris the Cat couldn't have said it better.

14 daily *Metroliner Service* trains are offered from New York to Washington

Watergate break-in takes place
June 17

Service is initiated to Vancouver, B.C., and Montreal

China designs are established and debut on the *Broadway Limited*

A new station opens in Cincinnati

Amtrak orders 40 new diesel electric locomotives

As it crosses the Bush River Bridge in Maryland in 1972, this northbound *Metroliner* is seen to have small Amtrak logos applied directly over predecessor Penn Central markings.

Amtrak photo

In 1972, Amtrak rolled out its first official paint scheme (known as Phase I) to bring a uniform look to its rainbow fleet. Here, workers apply the new scheme to an observation car.

Amtrak photo, John Carten collection

A crowd turns out to witness the experimental United Aircraft TurboTrain at Petersburg, Va. Amtrak inherited this TurboTrain from the U.S. Department of Transportation and operated a national tour in 1971 showing off the new technology. The articulated lightweight trainset featured gas-turbine propulsion and was designed to be the next major advance in high-speed passenger rail.

Doug Riddell collection

Amtrak lets a contract for design of new bi-level cars (later known as Superliners)

"Save Energy—Take *Our* Car" campaign targets consumers concerned about rising gas prices

Amtrak takes delivery of 40 SDP40F diesels and orders 110 more for delivery in 1974

June 22

Amtrak orders 57 *Metroliner*-type cars (later Amfleets)

March 29
American military withdraws its last soldiers from Vietnam

Amtrak appoints 2,300 additional travel agents, as well as 28 agents in West Germany, to sell tickets

New ticket reservation system is installed with a pair of computers in corporate headquarters

October 16
OPEC announces a 70 percent increase in the price of oil; average price of gasoline is 40.2 cents a gallon

John Carten collection

Inherited locomotives came in various states of mechanical condition and reliability, and Amtrak was in need of new motive power. Amtrak started taking delivery of its first brand new locomotives, the EMD-built SDP40F, in summer 1973. In this photo, the *San Francisco Zephyr* climbs Donner Pass, Calif., with a pair of SDP40Fs.

This concept drawing of an Amtrak station became the model for many early era Amtrak-built stations around the country.

Ordered in 1974, Amtrak's first locomotive with head-end power capability was the GE P30CH, wearing a paint scheme in this concept drawing that was not used.

Photo courtesy Kalmbach Publishing Co.

Interior Designer Martha Whitaker works on plans for an expanded passenger lounge in New York Penn Station.

Photo courtesy Kalmbach Publishing Co.

Amtrak's first National Operations Center opened in the early 1970s at L'Enfant Plaza in Washington, D.C. In the days before computer networks and GPS, train positions were manually tracked on a large magnetic map of the system.

Congress passes the Regional Rail Reorganization Act, which directs transfer of the Northeast Corridor to Amtrak
November 9

Reserved coach space, except for *Metroliner Service* trains, is done by specific seat assignment to facilitate group seating

First product, a 67 cent packet of Wrigley's Juicy Fruit gum, marked with a Universal Product Code (UPC) is sold
June 26

November 3
Amtrak purchases TurboTrains from Canada for service north of New York City

Planned new routes include Norfolk-Cincinnati, Boston-Chicago, Minneapolis-Duluth, Detroit-Jackson, and Washington-Denver

June 27
Ticketing and reservation system is completed and handles 78,000 calls a day

Amtrak photo, Matt Donnelly collection

New P30CH locomotive no. 700, the realization of the concept shown on opposite page, was purchased for intended use with Amfleet cars using head-end power.

Doug Riddell

Locomotive Engineer Robert MacDougald waits for the blue flag to be removed from his SDP40F locomotive at Richmond, Va., in 1977, so the *Silver Star* can speed across Virginia and the Carolina Piedmont to Raleigh, where another engineer will forward the 18-car train to Miami, Fla.

Amtrak photo, John Carten collection

A sleeping car attendant converts the seating space in one of his car's rooms into a sleeping berth to provide a comfortable bed for the evening's passengers.

Amtrak photo, John Carten collection

A school group boards an RTG Turboliner, Amtrak's first purchase of brand-new rolling stock, which went into service in 1973. These trainsets were a French design, powered by gas turbine engines similar to the technology used on the UA TurboTrains.

Jesse Padilla: Amtrak's Family Man

Growing up the youngest of seven, Jesse Padilla racked up the kind of workplace skills it has taken others years on the job to learn. Early on, he honed his own style of diplomacy: get results by being open. Be respectful. Jesse also learned that the best way to be heard is to speak up. Most importantly, he knew the support of a big family.

His 35-year career at Amtrak, he says, has shown him power of that kind of support. "Most of the people I still work with started at around the same time I did, so we have all grown up together," he says. "We really are a family." Over the years, his Amtrak family has helped him through some of the roughest patches of his life; he never thinks twice about giving back. "We all help each other," he says. "It just gets in your blood."

Jesse was 19 years old when he started working for Amtrak as a baggage handler in his hometown, San Antonio, Texas—and he didn't intend to stay. No one in his family had gone to college, and most worked in manual labor or maintenance (two of his older brothers worked for the railroad); Jesse had other plans. But when one of his older brothers started working at Amtrak, which had just taken over Southern Pacific Railroad's long-distance passenger operations in 1971, and recommended that he apply for a summer job there himself, Jesse figured there was nothing to lose. He quickly discovered, in fact, that the experience would open up new vistas.

"In the 30 days I worked there, I went from not knowing many people outside of Texas to meeting people from all over the country, even from around the world," he says. "I had never had those kinds of opportunities before, and it was really exciting for me to get to meet those folks, learn about their lives and travels, and introduce them to San Antonio."

So, when the summer stint was up, and Amtrak asked him if he'd like to work in Houston for a couple of months—with no promises for full-time work—he accepted. "It just kept rolling along like that," he chuckles, recalling his first years at Amtrak. "They'd offer me a short-term job in a different place in the Southwest, and I'd say, 'Okay, I'm ready!'"

Working his way up from baggage handler to ticket clerk to manager of customer service, Jesse was, in the late 1970s, accepted for the job of union representative by a railroad labor union and was sent to the George Meany Center for

Labor Studies in Maryland for training. The job, however, was short-lived. Labor was not a good fit: Jesse loved customer service, and he missed it. So he rejoined the Amtrak family ranks.

But it wasn't easy. In 1979, lines were cut, and Jesse's only option at Amtrak was to move his family to Texarkana, on the Arkansas border of Texas. The company didn't cover moving costs, so employees helped each other out. "We'd all just pitch in with moving, loading up our trucks and cars," he says. But Jesse didn't harbor resentments against the company. "Job cuts and layoffs are part of working for any big company," he says. "I've always appreciated that at Amtrak. We are given rights and protections so long as we do our job—and Amtrak recognizes a job well done."

Jesse knows it. When he was promoted to handling customer service in the Southwest, he worked hard not just to satisfy passengers but also to bring attention to his territory. "If I knew that the president [of Amtrak] was going to be in Texas, I always got on the phone and said, 'We'd sure like to meet you and to show you what we're doing,' and some came," he says. "I never hesitated to go to the top for anything because I have always believed that we really are like a family here."

That sense of unity, however, was dealt a blow in the mid-1990s, when Amtrak was divided into four different regional business groups. "That didn't work so well because this is a real people business," Jesse says. "We all had to compete for product lines, and customer care got lost in the shuffle." This fractious period of Amtrak's history coincided with the bleakest time of his

life: his 14-year-old daughter was suffering from kidney failure. In spite of Jesse's donating one of his kidneys to her, she died in 1993.

The Amtrak wagons circled. "A colleague sent out a message to people all over the country, and people—some I didn't even know—would call and say, 'I don't know what to say other than I was thinking of you,'" he says, pausing to remember that time. "At least 30 people from around the country came to my daughter's funeral." Jesse has two remaining children, Justin and Alexis.

Five years later, Jesse found himself seeing more problems arise within Amtrak, when the company announced that it would have to shut down four train routes including the *Texas Eagle*, the passenger line running from Chicago to San Antonio. "Train transportation is important for a lot of people who live along that line," Jesse explains. "Many of them can't afford plane travel, and they're traveling to places planes don't go to anyway." But the *Texas Eagle* was also losing money; Amtrak would need about $5.6 million to keep it running.

Jesse joined several of his longtime colleagues and met with mayors all along the *Texas Eagle*'s route; every mayor signed a petition to keep the train running. They took the petition to then-governor George Bush and made the case for the state to lend the necessary funds to Amtrak; the state agreed. "The mayors had to be cosigners on the loan," says Jesse. "But we saved the line through real grassroots community work." The *Texas Eagle* went on to make a million dollars in ridership revenue—thanks to the local revenue management team that Griff Hubbard, Bill Pollard, and Jesse launched with the local mayors coalition. Amtrak paid the loan off early in July 1999. His efforts that year won him recognition through the President's Service and Safety program, one of Amtrak's highest company accolades: the Award for Sustained Excellence.

Sustained excellence—just thinking about the amount and quality of work that one must produce over periods of time to earn that characterization is enough to sap the juice right out of most of us. "Well, they say if you find a job you love, you'll never work a day in your life," Jesse laughs. "Kids now just want to make a lot of money and switch jobs to do that, but I tell my kids that in the workplace loyalty can be a virtue." Especially when loyalty goes both ways.

Richard Nixon
resigns as
president
August 8

Train goes through Parkersburg, Cincinnati,
and Indianapolis and is combined with existing
service between Indianapolis and Kansas City

235 bi-level Superliner cars
are ordered for long-distance
trains from Pullman-Standard

Microsoft
Corporation
is founded
April 4

Travel agents sell $20 million
worth of Amtrak travel

110 new diesel locomotives are placed
into service, but no new passenger
cars are delivered

Penn Central repair
facility at Beech Grove
is purchased

Ken Miller

In the Amtrak reservation bureau in San Francisco, Amtrak Reservation Agent Alan Orchison (right) works alongside Southern Pacific employees in 1973. They are using what was known as "the wheel" to organize each date's handwritten train bookings.

Photo courtesy Kalmbach Publishing Co.

Moving away from pencil and paper, computers helped increase productivity and booking accuracy. Amtrak's Automatic Reservation and Ticketing System (ARTS) achieved full nationwide operation on June 27, 1974. By the end of that summer, the system handled 78,000 calls.

Robert LaMay

A TurboTrain sporting a bold Amtrak livery is seen heading towards New York while passing through Rocky Neck State Park along Long Island Sound in Connecticut.

Amtrak ❯❯
METROLINER

one of the fastest trains in the world

These famous posters that adorned the walls of travel agencies and stations across the country were made from watercolors painted by award-winning artist David Klein.

Joy Smith: Teacher of Many

In 1978, Joy Smith was 10 years into a career as a junior high school drama and public speaking teacher in Harlem, where she was born and raised. Then life threw her a curve ball. Frank, her husband of more than a decade, passed away—and the 34-year-old widow decided she needed to make a change. "I wanted to do something completely different," she remembers. "I wanted to be very busy. So I came to work at Amtrak."

A friend had tipped her off to an opportunity at Amtrak, where she was hired to be part of the dining crew onboard the *Crescent*, running from New York to New Orleans. "I must have been one of the oldest waitresses when I worked on that crew," she laughs warmly. "I had an absolute ball. It was a joy—not to pun on my name —to meet the old railroad men who made it all possible."

It was apparently a joy having Joy on staff as well. When her summer gig wound down, she was offered a position in the Washington, D.C., commissary, where all of the supplies, from food to sheets and pillows, are stored for the trains. She bid good-bye to chalkboards and erasers and headed south. "That was fun because it was almost like a hotel. I was learning all the aspects of the service: the front of the house, the back of the house."

An early career highlight came when she was working as a ticket clerk in Washington Union Station shortly thereafter. Alan Boyd, then the president of Amtrak, overheard her helping a customer and was impressed enough to commend her to her bosses. And just like that she found herself working in the "896" inventory control office, which accounted for the stock of food and beverages that went onto the trains and the receipts that came back. "That was a first quasi-taste of being somewhat in charge," she says. "I did a good job. We kept our debits down to a minimum."

But she missed working more directly with people. In 1981, she applied for, and got, a job back in New York as manager in charge of training employees for the Northeast Corridor. She excelled at teaching new ticket agents and onboard service and commissary workers. She developed new training programs and planned refresher courses for existing employees.

Her people skills were so valued that when Amtrak created the new onboard chiefs program in 1983, she was picked to help prepare men and women to work on the trains as liaisons between

the passengers and conductors and the rest of the staff. "I thought it was such an exciting job that I became a chief of onboard services," she recalls. "What a fantastic job that was. We were doing something new. We were going to make customer service the focal point."

She worked that job, riding the *Crescent* again, for nearly 10 years. But it was not without its initial complications. "You had guys who had been working there for a long time and it was definitely challenging to have a woman—and an African-American woman at that—come in and say 'I'm in charge of this train. I'm the new sheriff in town'," she says before adding without a pause: "It was absolutely fun. I learned a lot from those old conductors." Customer complaints went down along her route, she says, and compliments went up.

After returning to New York for a job on the crew base as manager of customer service—"too quiet for me; you miss the action of what's taking place on the train." Then in 1994, President Tom Downs introduced the Strategic Business Units (SBUs) at the railroad. Under the new regime, Joy moved to Chicago to become the product line manager for the *Texas Eagle*.

"We had our own little marketing group, our own little sales group; we would visit the various reservation call centers. We would design our logo for the trains. You had your own budget so that you could do pretty much what you thought you needed," she marvels. "We had our own little train."

When her boss, General Manager Don Cushine, took on a special assignment in Washington, D.C., she filled in as general manager of not only the *Texas Eagle* but

also the *Empire Builder* from Chicago to Seattle and Portland, the *California Zephyr* from Chicago to Oakland, and the *Southwest Chief* from Chicago to Los Angeles. Suddenly this former teacher had something in the neighborhood of 700 railroad employees reporting to her. "I was responsible for everything connected to those trains: the men and women, the mechanical people in the field, staying on budget, hiring and interviewing," she says.

She was also confronted with perhaps her greatest challenge yet. In November of 1996, Amtrak announced that it was going to discontinue the *Texas Eagle* along with the *Pioneer* and *Desert Wind*. That kicked off a year-long grassroots fight to save the line. Mayors along the *Texas Eagle* route lobbied Senator Kay Bailey Hutchison to extend funding to Amtrak. Joy traveled back and forth from Chicago to advocate for the railroad she loved.

"I felt I could not let Texas down," she says. "I was the fat lady. I didn't have a song, and I wasn't about to sing."

The relentless cheerleading of Smith, and many others, paid off. The *Texas Eagle* was saved. In recognition of her efforts, she was nominated by fellow colleagues for the prestigious President's Service and Safety Award.

Cushine would eventually take his old job back and the SBUs were abandoned in a return to a divisional structure. Today Joy is the superintendent of passenger services for the Central Division in Chicago.

Even after everything she's done with the company—living in New York, Washington, Chicago, Texas, and New Orleans—she has no plan to slow down. "The new president has ideas, vision," she says. "I'm just kind of excited. If someone had told me 35 years ago that I'd be working for a railroad, I'd say 'no way, Jose. I'll be a principal at some high school'."

And indeed, she's still teaching. Joy Smith sees her latest important role at Amtrak as a coach and mentor, "I am just so pleased when I look around this company and I see men and women in various positions and I had something to do with that," she marvels. "That just knocks me out. Makes me really happy inside. People are my passion."

At 69, she aims "to be of service and help my peers and subordinates reach their goals in this company. It's time to give back," she says. As if she hasn't given so much already.

4 Turboliners, 6 electric and 16 diesel-electric locomotives, and 115 new Amfleet passenger cars enter service
August 7

USA Rail Pass is introduced to overseas markets
November 1

Major program initiated to facilitate intermodal travel by providing reservation clerks with information on bus interchange routes

October 11
Saturday Night Live premieres on NBC

Budd Company turns out Amfleet cars at a rate of one per working day

Don Crimmin

On the southbound *Texas Chief* at Fort Worth, Texas, April 11, 1973, in the days before head-end power, refrigeration on this dining car was achieved by loading ice blocks through a hatch on the roof.

Amtrak photo, John Carten collection

While the locomotives take on fuel, this employee is filling the boiler's water tank. The steam generator located at the rear of this SDP40F diesel provided comfortable interior temperatures for the cars.

Amtrak photo, Matt Donnelly collection

Amtrak began upgrading its best Heritage equipment from steam heat to heat powered by more reliable electric head-end power. The program kicked off on May 26, 1977, at the Beech Grove maintenance facility.

Apple Computer
is founded
April 1

30 F40PH locomotives
are put into service

Amtrak acquires Keystone and
Springfield Lines and Michigan
Line (then 83 miles) from Conrail

United States
Bicentennial
is celebrated
July 4

Both President Ford and
Jimmy Carter make campaign
trips aboard Amtrak trains

April 1
Amtrak takes over Northeast Corridor with
direct control of trains and track forces,
dispatching, signaling, and maintenance

Amtrak takes over maintenance
facilities in Chicago, Detroit, Buffalo,
and the Northeast Corridor

Amtrak becomes the first national
company to offer reservation service to
passengers with hearing disabilities

Budd-built Amfleet cars and an EMD-built F40PH locomotive pose for a
publicity photo at Stonington, Conn. This equipment proves to be some
of Amtrak's most reliable yet.

Amtrak photo, Ann Owens collection

John Carten collection

A family heads down the platform to board
their train while a red cap collects their luggage
for loading.

Amtrak photo, Matt Donnelly collection

Amtrak's $15 million Turbo facility at Albany-Rensselaer, N.Y., was dedicated on November 30, 1977. The Americanized, Rohr-built
RTL Turboliners traveled at speeds up to 110 mph on the Empire Corridor for more than 20 years.

400 of the 492 Amfleet I cars go into service by the end of 1976

75 percent of day-service passengers travel in new Amfleet or Turboliner passenger cars

Jimmy Carter is inaugurated as president of the United States
January 20

Preportioned servings, frozen meal items, automatic beverage dispensing, and other modern preparation methods are employed

$1.75 billion Northeast Corridor Improvement Program (NECIP) kicks off
March 31

Corporate offices move to 400 North Capitol Street NW in Washington, D.C.

Amtrak implements automated Ticket-by-Mail system

May 25
Star Wars opens in theaters

Amtrak photo, John Carten collection

By the late 1970s, there was no mistaking which railroad was operating the *Metroliner Service*. This rebuilt Amtrak *Metroliner* set heads east through Metuchen, N.J.

Mike Schafer

Amtrak's RTG Turboliners were the mainstay on routes out of Chicago from the time they were delivered until being stored in 1981. Some were eventually upgraded to augment the *Empire Service* fleet and dubbed RTG-II Turboliners.

Amtrak photo, Matt Donnelly collection

In this 1978 photo of the interior of a Turboliner, the large picture windows offer a view of the magnificent scenery of the Empire Corridor, which paralleled the Hudson River for most of the trip.

Pat Willis: See Her Smile, Then Hear Her Roar

Like many young women in the early 1970s, Pat Willis didn't think she was ambitious. "Oh, Lord!" she says, laughing, "I never had a plan." When Amtrak hired this 28-year-old as a passenger service representative, and its 710th employee, in July 1972, she had no idea that she'd end up working there for 37 eventful years. Or that in the early 1980s, she would attain the title of train manager of the *Lake Shore Limited*. Or that at the end of her time at the company, she'd be able to say, "I was never bored in my entire life with Amtrak. It was always fun!"

Over the years, she broke a lot of ground, and shattered glass ceilings that were in place in every industry for women. Railroading was no different. In the early days of Amtrak, it was a male-oriented environment, and only a handful of women had jobs working on board the trains. In the 1970s, most of the employees were still working for various railroads under the Amtrak umbrella. One East Coast (New York to Florida) line employed female reps whose job description included modeling. Since it was the early '70s, the uniform for those female employees on Amtrak-run trains included short skirts and go-go boots. "I didn't have to wear them," says Pat, with audible relief.

It was a challenging environment for a woman but also for a girl who had grown up in a racially segregated world. She was "a white girl who grew up in a white neighborhood in Chicago." At Amtrak, she was surrounded by two groups of men: the African-American wait staff and Pullman porters, and the all-white conductors and engineers. It was a truly formative year. "I learned everything from the ground up," she says. "Mostly, I learned so much from those African-American men. Most of them were very highly educated, often with master's degrees, but when they were applying for jobs in the '40s, '50s, and '60s, one of the only jobs they could get was being a Pullman porter. This was a prestigious job providing status and access to a world others in the community couldn't reach. They bought homes and got their kids educated, and although there was a great deal of dignity associated

with the job, it was not unheard of to hear them be insulted. From those men, I learned that being effective in the service industry is an art form when done well."

Pat started out as a passenger service representative (PSR) based in Chicago, riding the train from origin to destination and back again, taking care of the customers, and working with the crew to make sure that problems on board were solved. Despite the racial and gender divides that were buffeting the country, on the trains, Pat recalls that relationships between men and women, black and white were cordial. "Everyone knew that they had a role (in keeping the trains running). They treated each other with respect and dignity within the confines of their work."

Not that it was always a smooth ride. This was the 1970s after all. The women who were flooding into the workplace were breaking new ground. Were they sexually harassed? "Of course. You just learned to wiggle out of it!" Traditional bathroom and sleeping arrangements had to be tweaked to suit the new dynamic. There was some initial squeamishness (especially on the part of the men), but the trains had to keep running, so, ultimately, everyone found ways to coexist.

With the passengers, however, there were always surprises. One night, Pat was sitting in the passenger section en route from Chicago to Kansas City when she saw a porter coming through the car, once, then twice, looking agitated. She asked him what was up. The porter said, "There's a man who wants me to find him company." Bewildered, Pat said, "What do you mean?" As people around her started to laugh, the porter repeated, "Pat, he wants me to find him company."

Knowing that a conductor was close by to rescue her if necessary, Pat went to the man's compartment and knocked on the door—hoping to set him straight. The man opened it, stark naked, welcoming, and very drunk. He merrily pulled her inside assuming that she was the company the porter had procured for him. Thanks to the conductor, Pat was able to

extricate herself. "The men who worked at Amtrak were always very kind to me," she says, "very protective." They shared a good laugh about it later.

In the early days, Amtrak had a start-up mentality: you didn't apply for jobs. You were assigned. There was no application procedure in place. That came a little later. You were assigned a job, you learned how to do it, and you did it. That might have alarmed some people, but not Pat, who was promoted to supervisor of PSRs after nine months. The position was ultimately expanded to include 40 PSRs and 15 tour escorts. When the Passenger Service Representative program was phased out, her job went too. The company offered no other positions and no severance. That was the system. But a manager who was in charge of onboard service and commissary operations in Chicago said, "She's a hard worker, I'll take her!" Pat found herself working in the commissary operation, making sure that the trains' dining and lounge cars were supplied with food and beverages and china, glassware, napkins, and silverware before leaving the station.

In 1975, just four years after she'd joined Amtrak, she was made general supervisor in Chicago Union Station. It was a huge responsibility in a station that was a major connection point. Pat and the two other people who shared the position were responsible for the station's entire passenger operation, from the ticket office and checked baggage area to the passenger lounge. She had to deal with delayed trains and accommo-

date passengers who had missed their connections (Chicago holds the distinction within Amtrak of processing more misconnected passengers than any other location in the system, both then and now), solve scheduling problems, and respond to the challenges of Chicago's winter weather. She relished it all, and when she went home, she always had entertaining stories to tell about the people and situations she'd encountered. "At social events, everyone wanted to hear my latest adventure!"

However exciting the work, it had its share of difficulties. In the late 1970s, Pat, then in her late 20s, found it awkward to supervise people who were much older and more experienced than she was. She had to learn how to be an effective supervisor while balancing everyone's interests. "You have to gain respect from them so that they will listen," she explains, "and you do that by listening to them." Then she told a story. She was on the night shift at Chicago Union Station and got a call from the man working at the information counter. This was a man who really knew the railroad in and out, well enough to have been a supervisor himself. He said, "I have a couple here who missed their train. It's their own fault, but they're nice people, older, and they're not from Chicago. I'd like to house them in a hotel for the night, even though it's not our policy." Pat thought for a moment and then said, fine. Looking back on it now, she says, "What I had just done was earn major stripes from him. He had realized in that moment that he and Pat shared a goal—to keep the passengers safe. That would be a hard call to make now, given today's thicket of regulations. "It certainly was pretty loosey-goosey then! But you could really grow, because you could make your own decisions."

Over the years, as a result of smart and thoughtful decisions she made, Pat rose steadily through the ranks and by the time she retired she was in a senior position with people reporting to her, men and women alike, counting on her to lead and mentor. It's been a long and rewarding journey for that young woman who "never had a plan."

Equipment shortages and failures, reductions in seat-miles operated, and delays in equipment delivery contribute to ridership drop

Heavy track work in Northeast Corridor includes first significant track mileage using concrete ties

First legal casino in the eastern United States opens in Atlantic City, N.J.
May 26

Joint station program incorporating local planning and financing is established for Wichita, Dallas, and other cities

Agreement is reached on operating *Southern Crescent* service between Washington and New Orleans via Atlanta

Amtrak is the only railroad consistently meeting industry's goal of 15 percent minority business participation

Amtrak photo

In late 1977, a growing Amtrak started moving its corporate offices from the L'Enfant Plaza location to 400 North Capitol Street NW in Washington, D.C.

Amtrak photo, Suzi Andiman collection

Amtrak officials inspect some of the first concrete ties installed by the new Track Laying Machine (TLM) at Shannock, R.I., in 1978 as part of the Northeast Corridor Improvement Project (NECIP).

Amtrak's Marketing department annually produced a number of compelling sales promotion pieces.

Interline agreements made with
12 new carriers increase the number
of cities served from 322 to 503

Amtrak contracts with Electro-
Motive Division for 15 high-speed
electric locomotives (AEM-7) for NEC

Amtrak launches
"We've Been Working on
the Railroad" ad campaign

61 stations
are completed
or rehabilitated

Travel agencies
contribute 14 percent of
total company revenue

September 17
Israel's Menachem Begin and
Egypt's Anwar Sadat sign the
Camp David peace accords

Congress sets two Amtrak goals: 55 mph
average system-wide speed and 50 percent
improvement in on-time performance

In 1978, Amtrak began installing concrete ties as part of NECIP in an effort to offer faster and more reliable service. The new TLM seen here in New England could replace up to a mile of rails and ties simultaneously per day.

			Passenger	
		Stations	**Miles**	**Revenue**
Fiscal Year	**Ridership**	**Served**	**(Millions)**	**(Millions)**
1971	6,450,304	—*	—*	—*
1972	15,848,327	440	3,038	170*
1973	16,958,056	451	3,806	200*
1974	18,670,319	473	4,258	256.9
1975	17,269,000	484	3,939	252.7
1976	18,046,136	512	4,155	277.8
1977	18,961,876	545	4,333	310*
1978	18,922,652	543	4,029	315*
1979	21,406,768	571	4,915	375

1970s

*Exact data not available

A chef prepares meals for hungry passengers in a brand new Superliner diner's kitchen. The air-conditioned, fluorescent lighted kitchen is outfitted with electric convection and microwave ovens.

Nuclear accident occurs at
Three Mile Island power
plant in Middletown, Pa.
March 29

Average price of
unleaded gas is
$1.04 a gallon

51 Superliners, the first
in a planned fleet of
284, are put in service

121 miles of track are rehabilitated including
the installation of 296,000 concrete ties and
74 miles of continuous welded rail

Congressional authorizes
$23 million for exclusive use
of state-supported services

Congress authorizes ordering of
a new generation of single-level,
long-distance cars

November 4
Iran hostage crisis begins as
U.S. citizens taken hostage at
American embassy in Tehran

Gary Pancavage

Amtrak GG1 no. 906 leads train 176 through Morrisville, Pa., in 1979.
An HEP car (second car) is required to supply power to the modern
Amfleet equipment in tow. This locomotive led Robert Kennedy's
funeral train from New York to Washington on June 8, 1968.

Blair Slaughter collection

This just-completed Superliner I sleeping car stands outside of the
Pullman-Standard plant. Superliner equipped trains are still the
mainstay for the majority of the long-distance fleet to this day.

Amtrak photo

In the late 1970s, Amtrak borrowed ASEA-built Swedish State Railways RC-4 electric locomotive no. 1166 in search for a
replacement for tired GG1 electrics and the unsuccessful E60s. It was numbered X995 and led to future orders for 53 AEM-7s.

As Amtrak moved into the 1980s, some old and troublesome equipment inherited from the freight railroads was being retired. F40PH no. 334 was delivered in July 1980 and remained in service into the next decade. Here, it poses for a publicity shot just outside Washington Union Station in Ivy City.

Amtrak photo, Matt Donnelly collection

Building a Dream

TURBULENCE, TURMOIL, AND TRAGEDY. Just as a teenager struggles to find his or her identity, Amtrak had to fight through growing pains to stake its claim in America's transportation network during its second decade. The 1980s for Amtrak were defined by financial instability, a recovering economy, and its first major derailment. But as the saying goes, "Whatever doesn't kill you only makes you stronger," and that was exactly the case for Amtrak.

The railroad made it through the 1970s, thanks in no small part to the two oil crises in that decade and the visionary people who formed the company. Those oil crises were bittersweet. They helped America remember why it needed passenger rail, and the recession that followed presented opportunities to acquire new equipment for the fleet at a good price.

The trains Amtrak was using were part of what was dubbed the Heritage fleet. And while they were considered solid equipment in their day, by the 1980s that day had passed. They needed to be updated. When the newly purchased Amfleet and Superliner cars were delivered, it gave Amtrak an opportunity to begin

Denny Sullivan

overhauling the Heritage cars. By extending their life, expanding the fleet, and offering customers new and improved equipment, it was possible for Amtrak to remain viable for years to come.

In the short term, though, the recession made it much harder to fill all those new seats.

One of the toughest things for the company to do early in its life was figure out how to run a fledgling railroad while managing some of the largest infrastructure projects Amtrak has ever completed. Congress had approved $2.19 billion to upgrade the Northeast Corridor in the late 1970s. With the planning and engineering

Bob VanderClute

work done, it was time to move dirt, lay track, and make things happen. Only the stability in the leadership ranks and the hard work of its dedicated employees kept the trains moving.

Chairman and President Alan Boyd put his people and political skills to great use. His ability to bring employees, contractors, suppliers, and government agencies together made it possible to operate and complete the Northeast Corridor Improvement Project without one interfering too much with the other. Though the project would take over a decade to complete, it is one of Boyd's biggest contributions.

Perhaps the only other piece of Boyd's legacy that rivals the infrastructure improvements is the core of managers he put in place. Melding a mixed group of managers from other railroads and industrial enterprises with service employees and young go-getters was no small task. Yet he was able to make it happen.

When World War II hero W. Graham Claytor Jr. came out of retirement to assume the role of president and CEO in 1982, he relied heavily on many of the men and women mentored by Boyd. Several of these leaders would eventually assume executive roles at Amtrak and guide the company for many years.

Claytor would need that leadership team as President Reagan's administration got up and running. Throughout its history, Amtrak has been plagued by unpredictable support and funding from the federal government. That was never truer than during the early 1980s.

Reagan wanted to shrink Amtrak's annual budget. Claytor was not opposed to cutting costs. Once, during a conversation about keeping costs in check, he relayed his philosophy on staffing. His view was that companies tend to add people over time, not all of which are truly necessary, so every four to five years it was probably a good idea to cut about 5 percent of staff to get back to the right headcount. By 1989, he had the company covering 72 percent of its operating budget, up from 48 percent when he took over. While not an ideal situation, this tightening of the purse strings made Amtrak learn to do more with less. That skill served it well in the long run.

Improving efficiency was tough. The company fought for new contracts to operate various commuter services. A partnership was formed with the U.S. Postal Service to transport mail and express packages. A massive restructuring of the route system took place to create cost efficiencies. And one of the most entrepreneurial endeavors was to leverage the right-of-way along the Northeast Corridor for an early MCI fiber optic network.

In concert with this business development, Claytor made sure that Amtrak was more focused on serving its passengers. The Passenger Services department was created with the goal of treating every passenger as a valued guest. Automated reservation centers were opened around the country to make booking travel on a train easier and faster.

Stations were treated as a priority too, because Claytor was concerned with improving the entire travel experience. Investments were made to renovate stations in Boston, Chicago, Dallas, Los Angeles, New York, Philadelphia, and Wilmington, Del. The most significant project by far was Union Station in Washington, D.C.

After a failed attempt to use the station as the National Visitor Center, which led to the station being abandoned and falling into disrepair, a powerful group of leaders in the nation's capital banded together to save the iconic building from the wrecking ball. Claytor, along with Secretary of Transportation Elizabeth Dole, Senator Daniel Patrick Moynihan, and Keith Kelly, who would become president of the Union Station Redevelopment Corporation, managed a complete renovation of the building and resurrected the station to the monumental status it deserves.

It was nearly a decade of hard work for many at Amtrak to complete that project. When it was reopened in 1988, Amtrak had a new corporate home, the capital city had a stately new transportation hub and vibrant shopping center, and local residents had the catalyst for much needed neighborhood redevelopment.

* * *

It was a Sunday. January 4, 1987. With the holidays just ending, many employees were at home or getting back in town from holiday travel. The phones started ringing. Our collective nightmare had become a reality. Maybe it's not as bad as it sounds. Hopefully the train was able to slow down first.

Assignments were given and many people jumped right into crisis mode as adrenaline took over. Some employees came unbidden to the office, others went to the site.

The first reports did not provide much information, only that there had been a collision. But as more information became available, it was apparent that things would change forever.

Colonial Train 94 had departed Washington Union Station on time at 12:30 p.m. headed for Boston. Engineer Jerome Evans piloted locomotive no. 903 with an additional locomotive and 16 cars full of passengers wrapping up their own holiday vacations in tow behind him. Just north of Baltimore, it happened.

Three Conrail locomotives were being moved from the company's Bayview Yard outside Baltimore to the Enola Yard in Harrisburg, Pa. The operator of the freight engines violated stop signals and proceeded on to the main line ahead of Train 94 in Chase, Md. At that point, the collision was unavoidable.

Train cars and locomotives were thrown—some crushed and some on fire. Helicopters, ambulances, police cars, and fire trucks arrived one after another. At the end of it all, 14 passengers and two crew members were dead. More than a hundred others were injured.

That incident became the defining moment of the decade for Amtrak. Out of the tragedy, however, numerous transformations took place that would improve not only Amtrak but the entire industry.

Amtrak management, its employees, and the Federal Railroad Administration all understood that changes had to be made to make sure something like this would not happen again. Many of the current federal requirements for certifying locomotive engineers, along with the safety technology used to control traffic on the railroad, are a direct result of that incident. Additionally, Congress passed legislation requiring mandatory drug testing for employees in safety critical jobs.

At Amtrak, internal changes were also made. When it was determined that the engineer operating the Conrail locomotive was under the influence of marijuana at the time of the collision, Amtrak created Operation Redblock (ORB). Still in place today, ORB makes it possible for employees in safety critical jobs to "mark off" from duty with no questions asked. It also creates a nonpunitive channel for employees to intervene with a colleague that is under the influence and get professional help if needed. Not only was this a huge step in safety, but it also improved relationships between Amtrak and its unions.

As the decade ended, Amtrak began to look to its future and contemplate how best to bring high-speed rail to the United States. However, those teenage years for Amtrak were difficult. But even though they were filled with turmoil and tragedy, there were also important triumphs. And the collective experience of the 1980s made the company a smarter and safer company.

Denny Sullivan worked in the railroad industry for 42 years and had 23 years of service with Amtrak, where he was an executive vice president and chief operating officer. He spent 10 additional years working for a railway maintenance equipment provider and on a high-speed rail project in Taiwan. He is now retired.

Bob VanderClute joined the Association of American Railroads as senior vice president Safety and Operations in 2003. In 1997, he joined Parsons Brinckerhoff (PB) as vice president and program area manager Rail after a 30-year career with the U.S. rail industry. Prior to PB, Bob was vice president Operations and chief operations officer of Amtrak. Other responsibilities with Amtrak included vice president of Customer Service, vice president of Transportation, general manager of National Operations, and general manager of the Northeast Corridor.

Complaints drop
40 percent over 1979

150 Amfleet II cars (125 long-distance
coaches and 25 food service cars) are
ordered from the Budd Company

February 27

Slumbercoach service is introduced
between Washington and Montreal
and Washington and Boston

Superliner I cars, the first new
long-distance cars in 2 decades,
are introduced on 4 routes

5 new state-supported routes are
established in California, Illinois,
Missouri, Oregon, and Pennsylvania

System Safety program designed
to train employees and reduce
injury rates is launched

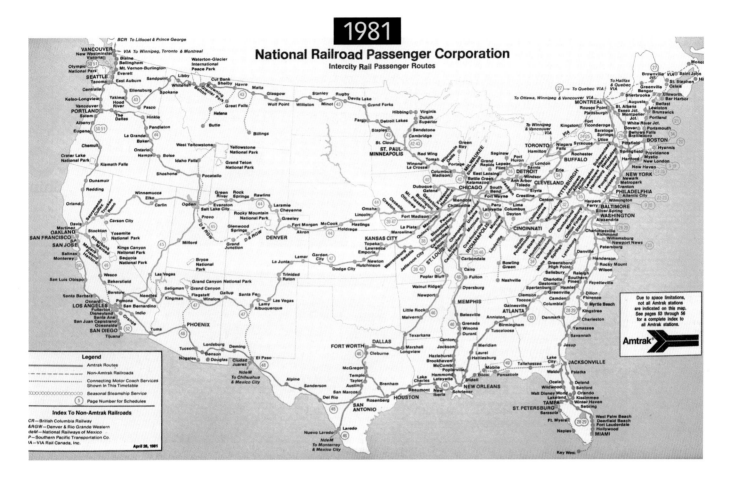

Construction on the parking garage is noticeable in this aerial photo of Washington Union Station as it undergoes renovation and rehabilitation into a transportation and retail center.

October 14

Staggers Act is passed, deregulating the railroad industry

Service quality improves, with customer complaints down 50 percent

January 20

Ronald Reagan is inaugurated as president, and U.S. hostages are released by Iran

Amtrak gains ownership of the Washington Terminal Company which operates train facility trackage within Union Station

December 8

John Lennon is assassinated in New York City

Long-distance trains register 11 percent ridership increase due to new Superliner equipment and improved on-time performance

Amtrak fleet includes 1,436 new or rebuilt all-electric passenger cars and fuel-efficient locomotives

April 12

First space shuttle mission takes place

Doug Riddell

Amtrak tested this Light Rapid Comfortable (LRC) trainset in 1980. The LRC featured tilting technology that allowed for faster speeds around curves. While none was ultimately purchased, this technology is used on today's *Acela* trainsets.

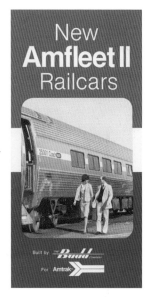

New **Amfleet II** Railcars

Amtrak started taking delivery of its new Amfleet II long-distance cars in 1981. These Budd-built cars came in coach and lounge configurations, supplementing and eventually replacing their Heritage fleet counterparts.

Amtrak photo

With the technological advances in a mainframe reservation system installed at Amtrak's reservation sales office in Bensalem, Pa., the company was able to close smaller, local reservation centers.

Express *Metroliner Service* (Washington-New York) trains make the trip in 2 hours 59 "civilized minutes" with a 92 percent on-time performance

Negotiations begin for installation of fiber optics system along the Boston-Washington right-of-way

Arrow, new nationwide ticketing and reservation computer system, is introduced

"See America at See Level" advertising campaign launches

23 AEM-7 locomotives are delivered

Corporate Development department begins to pursue asset utilization and diversification projects to generate additional revenue

AEM-7 locomotives enable trains to make Washington-New York run in 2 hours 49 minutes with 4 stops

Florida becomes the 8th state to participate in 403(b) program with daily Miami-Tampa round-trip service

Amtrak distributed 2000 prints of its 10th Anniversary logo in 1981.

New AEM-7 (left) and E60 (right) electric locomotives are at the Ivy City facility located north of Washington Union Station. These locomotives became the replacement for the venerable GG1 in the early 1980s.

As part of NECIP, new rail was laid to replace the worn-out rail inherited from the freight railroads, such as here on Track 1 around the curve in Branford, Conn.

43

Solomon Carey: Designated Commencement Speaker

Solomon Carey is nearing retirement after a 38-year career on the railroad and has become the designated commencement speaker for newly hired conductors.

In 1973, Solomon was 22, and living with his parents in Virginia Beach, Va. They had given him an ultimatum: be back in college by next week or get a job. He called his cousin Dennis, who was in the same hapless situation, and Dennis said, "I got us a job on the railroad!"

The two young men went to Baltimore to be interviewed for a freight job on the Penn Central Railroad. (Three years later, Penn Central and other freight railroads were consolidated into Conrail.) "The trainmaster said, 'Listen, guys, I can promise you that you will be hired if you want to work because we have a government mandate to meet.' He was talking about affirmative action. I'm saying, man, this looks so hard." The trainmaster reassured Solomon and Dennis. "He says, 'You throw a lot of switches out there, you make a lot of money. You won't work a hard day in your life.'"

It was an idyllic time. "We were 'extra boards,'" says Solomon, "relief conductors to step in when the regular ones took off." They loaded barges to ship from Cape Charles, on Virginia's Eastern Shore, across Chesapeake Bay. "Maybe a half hour or hour into the shift, a boat would come into dock, and we would shove a train onto it. We shifted the cars that we pulled off and took them to the little industries down there, and then we were done. We'd sit on the edge of the dock and go crabbing."

Within the year, Solomon was on his way up, promoted to conductor and working in Washington. For the next decade, it was all about freight. "The work was physical but very rewarding," he says. "You did a job well and finished. The little carrot was that one day you'd work the Amtrak *Metroliner Service* out of Union Station, and those were the gravy jobs. You didn't get dirty; you got to wear a uniform and look nice. You took the money and gave the tickets. That's how most freight conductors thought of it."

Solomon laughs heartily, explaining that when he became a conductor on Amtrak passenger trains in 1984, he learned how misguided that idea turned out to be. "Little did they know that the hardest part is not shifting cars, it's dealing with people. That's the toughest job anywhere, anyplace!"

It turned out to be Solomon's passion—as exciting to him as conducting classical choral music, which he does in his spare time. He compares the rewards of the two: "It really is amazing to see the reaction in the faces of the choir members once you've worked hard for months to produce a concert. When everything comes together, and it brings the audience out of their seats to a standing ovation, there is no better feeling." On the train, he tells the new hires, "The conductor is the iconic image of Amtrak. You're influencing 78,000 people a day, 190,000 if you include the commuter lines! It was my mantra that you had to wow these people who are making judgments about you and the corporation."

Solomon had his share of testing moments. Once, a seven-year-old child was accidentally abandoned on a train out of New York's Penn Station. It turned out that his mother had fled an abusive husband with the boy and a baby girl and had gone to make a quick phone call to her sister in Washington, D.C., when the train left without her and the baby. As Solomon gradually eased the story out of the distraught little boy, he was aware that everyone around was listening and concerned. He reassured the child, got him some food, settled him, and contacted Penn Station. Then, having decided that the boy would go to Washington and meet his mother there, he put him to work, helping take tickets. "A young lady said to me, 'How many kids do you have?' I said, 'None.' She replied, 'What a loss for some kid not to have you as a father!'

A potentially more disruptive situation occurred when a very large, mentally disturbed and aggressive-seeming man arrived on the train without a ticket and began pacing. Solomon geared himself up to deal with it. "Conductors have a

certain rhythm, almost never stopping, just moving forward to meet that other conductor. When that's interrupted, people stop talking or reading the paper; they want to hear the confrontation."

The big man started to shout. "I knew he was going to hit me and send my hat flying." A woman hugged her baby tight and left the car. Solomon quietly arranged for the police to meet the train at Philadelphia and then soothed the man, letting him walk around the train unaccosted. "Never get too proud about someone 'besting' you in front of passengers," Solomon says today.

This finely honed instinct for passenger service led Solomon to the crowning achievement of his career: the transfer bridge, used when a train breaks down and the passengers have to be taken off and placed on another train. In the past, they had to climb down the stairs to a steep step to the ground, walk across often uneven ground to the rescue train, and then climb up a second steep bottom step. Solomon says, "It was all kinds of people with their baggage going through just two or three doors, and at the other end, you had to push people right up to the ladder's bottom step, which was so high that it might come up to your chest." The procedure was embarrassing, awkward, and time consuming, and for years, Solomon felt that there had to be a better way.

The solution presented itself in 2008, when new *Acela Express* trains were designed with beautiful fiberglass bridges instead of

steps. Unfortunately, the *Northeast Regional Service*, on which most breakdowns occur, didn't receive the bridges. "I was on two trains in two days that needed transfers," Solomon says, "and when I got back to work, I said, 'This is it! We will have transfer bridges on *Regionals*.'"

By this time, he was program manager for onboard service, and, relying on the influence and goodwill that he had created over the years, he got on the phone. "The beauty of it was that having done transfers so many times, I knew exactly what it entailed." He ended up working with Environmental Health and Safety and the Equipment Engineering group in Wilmington, and after almost two years, it was done. Solomon is especially proud of the fact that their bridge is compliant with the Americans with Disabilities Act. "So far the bridges have transferred just over 4,000 people," he says proudly, "and that's why they gave us the President's Service and Safety Award for safety this year."

He says he'll never regret his move from operations to customer service. "In the old days, the thinking was freight thinking: we're moving cargo, and the cargo happens to be people. Now it's all about making people comfortable. If you have a vision for service, everyone else on the crew will have the motivation to deliver it. That's what I tell the young people and the real beauty of it all is to have those young men and women come up to me on the train and say, 'I really remember your talk, and I'm going to do it.'"

Menus expand, and
tablecloths, flowers,
and flatware return

Sleeping car service is enhanced with
morning coffee/tea, newspaper, and
complimentary shoeshine

EPCOT Center
opens in Florida
October 1

November 13
Vietnam Veterans Memorial is
dedicated in Washington, D.C.

Dining car
reservation
system is added

Joint Labor/Management
Productivity Council is
established

"All Aboard America"
advertising campaign
and fare plan begins

In an effort to improve the financial performance of passenger trains, new cars were purchased in 1986 to handle mail for the U.S. Postal Service. Mail handling cars were added either to the head end or rear end of trains and were worked en route during station stops.

John Carten collection

Matt Donnelly collection

In 1983, the last Amfleet II cars were delivered. Amfleet II lounge cars quickly became the center of social activity aboard single-level, long-distance trains.

THE FASTEST WAY TO GET YOUR SHIPPING COSTS DOWN TO EARTH

Amtrak Package Express

In addition to hauling mail, Amtrak also advertised shipping services. While U.S. mail is no longer carried aboard trains, Package Express service is still offered.

502 track-miles of continuous welded rail and 397 miles of concrete ties are installed in Northeast Corridor; speeds top 100 mph

Sally Ride becomes the first American woman in space
June 18

1-800-USA-RAIL begins

The number of travel agents offering Amtrak tickets tops 10,000 for the first time

Auto Train service expands from tri-weekly to daily operation

Major station rehabilitations are underway in Baltimore, Wilmington, Trenton, and Newark

Onboard chief program is established to place supervisors on long-distance trains

July 16
California Zephyr is rerouted from Wyoming through Denver over Moffat route

October 23
U.S. Marine barracks in Beirut are destroyed by a suicide truck bomb, killing 241 Marines

On October 30, 1983, Amtrak restored *Auto Train* service between Lorton, Va., and Sanford, Fla., Amtrak Train 53, the southbound *Auto Train*, crosses over Neabsco Creek, just south of Woodbridge, Va. This photo became a postcard used in the "All Aboard Amtrak" campaign.

Automobiles rode in fully enclosed auto carriers such as the one pictured here. *Auto Train* is the longest passenger train in the world, with two engines and 40-plus passenger railcars and auto carriers.

The loading and unloading of automobiles from multilevel auto carriers is carried out like a well-orchestrated symphony, as seen at the Lorton, Va., terminal.

1984

Bell System
breakup begins
January 1

New stations open in Anaheim,
Oceanside, Galesburg, Tacoma, Omaha,
Huntington, and New Carrollton

January 24
Apple Macintosh is released

Teletrak launches and provides
travel agents with an instant link
to Amtrak sales agents

Amtrak photo, Ann Owens collection

Instead of traditional dining car service on the *Auto Train*, buffet cars were used to accommodate the large number of passengers on this popular service.

Amtrak photo

A dining car crew loads food into the kitchen of a Super-liner diner, which was located on the lower level to free up the length of the upper level for dining passengers.

Amtrak photo, Matt Donnelly collection

Self-propelled SPV2000s could be operated from either end. They were designed to economically transport passengers on lines with lighter ridership without the need for separate locomotives and cars. The state of Connecti-cut owned 13 of these railcars that were operated by Amtrak between New Haven, Conn., and Springfield, Mass., in the early 1980s.

Curtis Dilly: Practical Poet

Curtis Dilly isn't much of a talker. It's not that he isn't polite. He'll certainly answer all your questions with a decorous "yes, ma'am" or "no, ma'am" in the manner befitting a Southerner who served in the Marine Corps. It is rather that, as in all endeavors, Curtis thinks things out before producing rough-cut gems; even his comportment, with his meticulously coiffed hair and goatee, bear that out. So, when you urge him to elaborate on the years of his work as a machinist and in-house tinkerer at Amtrak that led to an invention that has significantly improved the railroad's safety record—and for which he won Amtrak's 2007 President's Service and Safety Award—expect a stumped silence at first. Wait for the reply: "Well, ma'am, I don't know. I'm a man, we like to see how things work."

Anyone with a genius for a particular kind of thinking, it seems, finds it excruciating to explain how and why he does things. Curtis is no different. "I guess I always had a knack for taking things apart to see how they worked, getting ideas for how they might work better," he says, in his laconic, native West Virginian cadence. "But when you're young, it seems like the things you have a knack for, you don't feel much like doing."

What the very young Curtis did feel like doing was working for the railroad when he grew up. Riding his bike alongside the road that ran parallel to the train tracks in his hometown of Oak Hill, W.Va., he'd hear the sound of the train's whistle, and he says it would just take him somewhere in his mind. Locomotives, in particular, captured him. "There was something like a mystery about them," he says. "The way they looked, the way they worked, where were they going, where were all the people going— there was something big about it."

But by the time he was out of school, joining the United States Air Force seemed bigger than the railroad; Curtis dreamed of becoming a pilot. After about a year of service, however, the Air Force didn't seem big or gritty enough. In fact, he says, it seemed rather too gentlemanly. "I wanted something rougher, tougher, cooler," he says.

So he joined the Marine Corps, where he not only honed his gutsiness but also racked up plenty of experience not in an airplane but as a machinist. After he left the Marines in 1979, he went to school to study diesel engines—and a few years later, he was working for Amtrak in Washington, D.C., as a machinist's helper.

Over the years, Curtis couldn't help but notice minor engineering bugaboos that stuck in his craw. He'd ruminate on how various tools and systems might be constructed more efficiently so often, he says, that he can't even recall specifics of any of his ideas now. It wasn't until both his and his colleagues' safety became an issue that in 2001 Curtis made up his mind to draw up his own plans for what would become known as the Dilly Bar.

Working on Amtrak's high-speed rail service out of Washington, D.C., the *Acela Express*, Curtis and his fellow machinist technicians often had to lift open the train's nose cone, the snout-like apparatus on the forward-most section of the train, aerodynamically designed to cut through the air at top speeds. But as they worked under it, the 240-pound nose cone would sometimes suddenly snap shut, trapping workers underneath it—or partially underneath it. Once when Curtis was working in a plastic fiber suit in the middle of an insufferable mid-Atlantic summer, a nose cone fell and pinned his arms and legs; it was hours before help arrived. That was the last straw. "You get trapped in a nose cone enough, and believe me, you want to do something about it," he says.

Off hours, Curtis started giving serious thought to what kind of tool he'd need to support the nose cone to keep it from falling. When he'd come up with a clear idea—a specially designed bar that would grip the contours of the nose cone—he approached his supervisor, who was so impressed that he urged higher-ups at Amtrak to contract with the Washington-area machine shop Allen-Mitchell & Co. to produce a prototype based on Curtis' specifications.

At the time, many of Curtis' coworkers exhorted him to patent his plans, go into private business, and market the product himself. He thought about it, but came up with another idea instead. "After I gave the specs on the tool, I said to my supervisor, 'Tell you what— why don't you put the words "Dilly Bar" right there on it,'" says Curtis. "When I saw my name on that prototype, I thought, 'Now, that looks real good.'" The Dilly Bar underwent rounds of testing before Amtrak placed a major order in the mid-2000s. It has been used ever since throughout Amtrak's Northeast Corridor.

Curtis is still tinkering. For the past year and a half, he's been fiddling with a spring rig invention that would help lift spring coils from the trucks to the high-speed rail lines. "When I get it where I want it, that's when I'll show it," he says, with characteristic prudence.

But in all these years, Curtis hadn't stopped dreaming of flying. He'd sit on the back porch of his home in Harper's Ferry, W.Va., watching planes and waxing romantically and scientifically about them—to the extent, he says, that his wife (and mother of their four children) finally got "sick of it" and saved up to buy him flying lessons in nearby Frederick, Md. Today, he is finally a pilot, renting a Cessna 172 whenever he can drum up the spare money and time.

"When you see the sky up there from a different angle, it's like nothing you ever dreamed," he says. "The stars, all sparkling there in the night sky—they really are just like diamonds." Another rough-cut gem from the inventor of the Dilly Bar.

Amtrak acquires the remaining 50 percent interest in Chicago Union Station

Employee safety achieves the best level in Amtrak's history to date

Tickets are offered through the TWA and American Airlines ticket reservation systems

Enhancements aboard the *Southwest Chief* include guides, souvenir menus, games, and movies
May 1

Amtrak and Long Island Rail Road agree to share in modernization of New York Penn Station

The *Beech Grove*, the most advanced track geometry car in the country, is placed in service

January 28
"We Are The World" is recorded in Hollywood

March 11
Mikhail Gorbachev becomes leader of the Soviet Union

27,000 travel agencies can process Amtrak ticket sales through the Airline Reporting Corporation

Amtrak photo, John Carten collection

In 1984, damaged Amfleet Coach 21222 was rebuilt into an office car for Amtrak officials, renumbered 10001, and named *Beech Grove* in honor of the maintenance facility that rebuilt the car.

Alex Mayes, Kalmbach Publishing Co. collection

On October 28, 1984, the inaugural run of Train 86, the Richmond, Va., to New York *Virginian* begins as the train pulls out of Richmond at 7 a.m.

Amtrak photo, Blair Slaughter collection

The 10001 featured an area in the rear where officials could inspect the railroad. It was also equipped with bedrooms, a dining area, and a kitchen.

NOT EVERYONE WAS MEANT TO FLY

ALL ABOARD AMTRAK

Notable marketing campaigns from the 1980s featured the slogan "America's Getting into Training" as seen on several of these posters. Some of the posters also highlight the scenic rewards of train travel.

rediscover washington

discover Amtrak

We've been working on the Railroad bringing you low excursion fares, tours, the U.S.A. Rail Pass and many more exciting programs. Let Amtrak or your Travel Agent give you all the details, now!

AMTRAK'S NEW SUPERLINER. THE SUPER WAY TO SEE AMERICA AT SEE-LEVEL.

AMERICA'S GETTING INTO TRAINING

51

Ed Vogel: Protector of the Little Guy

Growing up on a farm in Jessup, Md., Ed Vogel was never all that interested in trains. The automobile was his first love. But the rails are in his blood: his father was an engineer and his grandfather, a conductor for the Baltimore & Ohio Railroad (B&O).

His rural upbringing instilled in Vogel a work ethic and sense of fairness that would see him through several stages of a career at Amtrak: as a brakeman, in labor relations, as ombudsman, and now in the inspector general's office. "Growing up on a farm, we didn't have a lot of money," says Vogel, the oldest of five. "But my parents put us through Catholic grade school and high school. Private school. Every one of us. They found the money. It was always about doing the right thing and standing up for what is right."

His initial experience of railroad life, though, was not promising. In 1967, the summer after his freshman year at Bowie State, he went to work for three months as a brakeman on the B&O. "I almost got killed twice," says Vogel, who is now 62. "In those days, when you worked, you heard jingling in the pockets of the other brakemen. It was liquor. I almost got coupled. I almost got rolled."

Instead, he decided to pursue his passion—cars—and, in 1968, went to work for General Motors in a parts warehouse. By 1976, it was clear that the path he was on wasn't going anywhere, so he consulted with his father, who urged him to reconsider trains and take a job at the B&O. "He said you could have a good career in the railroad," recalls Vogel. At his father's urging, the younger Vogel reached out to the vice president of Labor Relations who urged him to get more practical experience first. So Ed Vogel went to work as a conductor.

Two years later, though, he had landed a job in labor relations for B&O. He was recruited by a former colleague who had joined Amtrak's productivity and improvement group. His fellow B&O employees scoffed at his career choice. "They said, 'Why would you want to go work for a company that doesn't make any money?'" laughs Vogel. "I wanted to get a variety of experiences and improve my skill sets. I worked that job for about 18 months and then Reagan got elected. He said in his State of the Union speech that he was going to get rid of Amtrak. So they had a reduction in force. I got RIFed. The whole department was abolished."

His old boss at B&O refused to take him back in labor relations, so Vogel returned to the rails—taking a job as a conductor

there, which he says he "loved." But the hours were long, and after three years, Vogel was contacted by Amtrak again and invited to return as a labor analyst. He took the job in 1984 and never looked back. "I was excited to get back into management and do something with my education," he says. "I had met a lot of people in the months I was there. Amtrak is a company that, if there's ever an underdog, is the underdog. I had come to understand there were a lot of really good, competent and talented, really nice professional people. It still gets reinforced in me every day."

That spirit of valuing each contribution—and feeling protective of the little guy—did not go unnoticed by Vogel's superiors. In 1992, he became the ombudsman of the company, a position that he calls "the high point of my career. I was an advocate for the employees who needed an advocate. You can be a resource for someone who maybe has a bad boss or something happens that's not fair. You get to do really good work in the name of the president's office and you represent Amtrak in that way."

At least one of the things he is most proud of is something he may not even have been technically allowed to do. A woman who worked as an engineer in Portland, Ore., was stricken with cancer in 1993. She couldn't work, and her bills were mounting at an alarming rate. Her family was supportive but could only do so much. "They asked if there was anything we could do to help her," says Vogel. So with the Payroll department, he helped set up a bank account into which other employees could donate their vacation days. "We probably broke a bunch of railroad retirement laws, but she ended up with a couple hundred vacation days that she was able to take and be paid for and

ultimately come back and keep her job. We didn't broadcast it; we did it undercover and we were able to help her out."

That attitude—individualism with a bent towards justice—continues to serve Vogel in his current work as chief of inspections and evaluations for the Office of Inspector General (OIG). The department of approximately 100 people serves as the company watchdog, funded through Congress and totally independent, says Vogel, "to be on the lookout for waste, fraud, and abuse."

One of his most wide-ranging investigations began in 2002 when OIG investigators found a series of revenue discrepancies: the number of tickets issued and the income reported were not matching up. The same was happening with food and beverage sales. In short, employees who handled cash were stealing from Amtrak. "The company had gone through major reorganizations, and they lost track of the day-to-day operations of ticketing and the food and beverage sales," he says. "People were stealing because there was opportunity and greed. There were all kinds of scams."

The bad apples who were exploiting lax oversight were not only costing the railroad money, says Vogel, they were also creating a hostile work environment. "There's a lot of peer pressure out there: do you rat the person out or do you turn the other way? You shouldn't have to work with that. We didn't want the good employees to work next to a thief. Our employees deserve to be able to come to work and do their job."

So Vogel and the OIG put together teams from the Customer Service, Operations, Transportation and Finance departments to dig into the problem. Over the course of four years, 500 people throughout the company were implicated and let go. "We got back to the basics," says Vogel.

Vogel demurs at the slightest suggestion that any work he's done for the company approaches remarkable. For him, he says, what matters is "always trying to find the truth and making sure that it is invoked. It's bringing some fairness into everyday life the way it was intended, whether it was a policy or a procedure or a program."

Soon, Vogel says he will retire. He's returning to his first love: cars. He will leave Washington with his wife and move to Charleston, S.C. "There's a local Maserati dealership there," he says. "I'm going to get a job selling Alfa Romeos and Maseratis, so I can lease one of those and drive it every day to and from work." After loving cars and working on trains, it's only fair.

Amtrak purchases a maintenance facility in Bear, Del.

Amtrak takes over completion of NECIP from the Federal Railway Administration

Custom class is introduced on the *San Diegans*

Loss of the Challenger space shuttle occurs
January 28

January 20

Executive Sleeper service is Inaugurated on the *Night Owl* for Washington-New York business travelers

Track upgrades of the Northeast Corridor and Michigan Line include resurfacing 436 miles of track

First celebration of Martin Luther King Day takes place

Amtrak photo, Ann Owens collection

F40PH locomotives and Superliners were used on the majority of long-distance trains in the west throughout the 1980s. An eastbound train is traveling along the Columbia River in Washington.

Amtrak photo, Matt Donnelly collection

Amtrak performs heavy overhauls and repairs at the Beech Grove shops outside of Indianapolis. Here a wreck-damaged F40 locomotive is getting a nose job and will soon be back on the road.

Amtrak photo, Blair Slaughter collection

In 1985, the original RTG TurboTrains from France were rebuilt and modernized. Part of the upgrade included modifying the nose of the power cars to match the later RTL Turbos.

Amtrak passes Eastern Airlines to become the leading Washington-New York carrier

Service is added to Cape Cod during the summer months

Construction begins on Washington Union Station redevelopment led by the Union Station Redevelopment Corporation

Route guides, movies, games, and a hospitality hour are added to the *Empire Builder*, *California Zephyr*, and *Coast Starlight*

Complimentary meals are introduced for sleeping car patrons

Railfones becomes available on *Metroliner Service* trains, allowing passengers to place calls to people outside the train

"A-plus" system allows customers to purchase tickets over the phone and pick them up at the station

Hourly *Metroliner Service* from Washington to New York resumes

Modification of electrical equipment begins on Amfleet cars to allow trains to operate in push-pull service

John Carten

In the 1980s, newer technologies made business more efficient. Here, a passenger uses a self-service ticketing machine at New York Penn Station to purchase a ticket instead of waiting in line.

Amtrak photo, Matt Donnelly collection

This engineer intently looks ahead, with one hand on the throttle and the other on the horn valve of this 260,000-pound F40 locomotive.

Amtrak photo, Matt Donnelly collection

With the remainder of the Heritage fleet nearing the end of its useful life, in 1988, Amtrak developed and built two new prototype sleepers known as Viewliners. After testing, they would eventually result in an order for 50 cars in the 1990s.

Amtrak photo, Blair Slaughter collection

The interior of the Viewliner sleeper was equipped with a large accessible bedroom that enabled passengers with disabilities to travel in spacious sleeper car space.

Amtrak publishes 92-page travel planner of all the trains, accommodations, and hotel and tour packages available

First *Simpsons* cartoon airs on the *Tracy Ullman Show*
April 19

First Viewliner prototype is completed

January 4
Amtrak Train 94 collides with 3 Conrail locomotives at Chase, Md., resulting in 15 fatalities and 174 injured

Construction begins on expanded *Auto Train* terminals at Lorton and Sanford

June 12
President Reagan challenges Mikhail Gorbachev to tear down the Berlin Wall

John Carten collection

In 1987, the first Centralized Electrification and Traffic Control (CETC) center opened in Philadelphia. Train dispatchers used computers to control the routing of trains rather than issuing instructions to local control towers along the railroad.

Doug Riddell

Even with CETC, many control towers along the railroad still did things the old fashioned way. In 1986, Operator Jack Robertson is seen preparing train orders at Washington Union Station.

Doug Riddell

Conductor Jerry Maxey and Assistant Conductor Denise Ring prepare to board their train in Washington, D.C., and will take it to Richmond, Va.

Ira Silverman: Doing It All Except Punching the Ticket

During the 1980s, one Amtrak vice president called Ira Silverman "the conscience of Amtrak." Another said that every company needed an Ira Silverman. Still another simply called him "Mr. Amtrak." All of these were accurate reflections of how his role transcended his title—director of Route Marketing.

When Amtrak created the Route Marketing group, its objective was to determine the marketing actions and other steps needed to compete effectively and increase revenues. In selecting Silverman in 1980 to lead the effort, the company chose the man whose energy, creativity, railroad knowledge, personal credibility, and love of trains led him and his department to be the catalyst for so much of what Amtrak accomplished over the next 15 years.

It was as if Ira had been preparing for that job his whole life. As a youngster in Queens, N.Y., his burning passion for trains frequently led him to New York Penn Station to watch the great streamliners depart. He worked summers as a ticket agent on the Long Island Rail Road, and in college, he even did a stint as a block operator for the Elgin, Joliet & Eastern Railroad.

As a teenager, inspired by his visits to Penn Station, he had developed a new schedule pattern for the Pennsylvania Railroad's New York to Washington line and sent it to the railroad's president. Although he never got a response, years later, it would be the same New York-Washington route where Ira would leave his first big mark on Amtrak. The success of the *Metroliners* in the early 1970s had deteriorated along with the New York-Washington tracks when the Penn Central Railroad fell into bankruptcy. During the second half of the decade, the Northeast Corridor Improvement Project gradually rebuilt the railroad, but at the price of slower schedules and poor reliability for several years. The first big challenge facing Silverman and Route Marketing was to come up with a plan to rebuild the lost *Metroliner* ridership. Added into the mix was airline deregulation, which spawned low cost airfares between major urban hubs. The challenge was formidable.

Silverman knew that just running the trains faster and on time, while essential, would not be enough to reestablish *Metroliner*'s previous success. Silverman and his team brought together all the company departments, and spurred on by Silverman's enthusiasm, knowledge, and frequent cajoling, a plan to resurrect the *Metroliner Service* took shape.

The rough-riding, self-propelled *Metroliner* cars would be replaced by much newer, locomotive-hauled Amfleet cars. Low-density seating would offer more leg room, and dinette cars with tables would provide work areas for business travelers. Three limited-stop express trains would restore the under three-hour schedule that had been *Metroliner*'s hallmark. Amtrak would emphasize these amenities as offering a more comfortable and productive way to travel. Operations and Passenger Services delivered on-time performance and consistent onboard service. The market began to return, and over the next two decades, *Metroliner Service* flourished. It carried more passengers than the air shuttles until being replaced by the next generation high-speed train, the *Acela Express*.

Western long-distance trains had begun receiving brand new Superliner equipment starting in 1980, but low-fare air service was spreading around the country. When one could fly from Chicago to the West Coast for $79, it was tough for Amtrak to compete. With ridership slipping, it was again Silverman and his team that developed a plan to do what the competition could not. Instead of just offering transportation, the western Superliners would become land cruises. In 1984, the *Southwest Chief* was the first train to get the new package of onboard games such as bingo, happy hours, evening movies in the lounge car, printed route guides, and even a guide who rode across parts of New Mexico and Arizona to explain the area's culture and history. And for people who came off of eastern trains and had several hours to wait in Chicago, there were sightseeing tours. Certainly no airline could do that! The up-

graded service was promoted, and soon ridership began to recover. Before long, Silverman's land cruise concept was launched on most long-distance trains.

But it wasn't just the big projects that characterized Silverman. He traveled every Amtrak train and route he could, taking the temperature and pulse of the Amtrak product. He talked to passengers, ticket agents, train and engine crews, reservation agents, onboard attendants, and vice presidents. Silverman listened to anyone, and if they had a good idea, he and his staff would carry it forward.

In addition to listening closely to others, Ira saw things that others didn't. Late in fall, the first time he would enter an Amfleet restroom, the annual "cold bathroom" memo would go out. After many years of sending the memo, changes were made to bring more heat into the bathrooms. Silverman knew that big ideas alone wouldn't work unless the everyday details were taken care of so that the passengers would enjoy their trip. And he knew that communication was vital. Part of every plan coming out of his department was how the details and rationale were to be explained to the employees on the front lines who had to deliver the product.

Ira was the head of the Timetable Committee and also spent much of his time on and off the job looking to improve schedules to better utilize equipment, enhance

connections, and increase ridership by improving times at key locations. His staff often commented that "Ira never met a schedule he didn't want to change."

Even though he was such a key person at Amtrak through the mid-1990s, that didn't keep him from pitching in to work in Union Station on Thanksgiving weekend handling the crowds, going on the road to man equipment displays at Amtrak's Family Days, or leaving a train stuck behind a freight derailment to go to a nearby grocery store and buy food for the passengers. As one route manager on his staff said, "Ira would go out there and punch the tickets and expect us to do the same thing, if that's what it took to get something done." From that came The Ticket Punch Award, which Ira awarded to people throughout the company who had helped on a Route Marketing effort. Appropriately, it had a picture of a conductor's ticket punch and the sentiment: "For doing it all short of punching the ticket."

Ira gives much of the credit for his success to the team that he assembled. "The route managers, project managers, and my administrative assistant Jacqui Beigie, all were enthusiastic, creative, and committed to what we were trying to do. Many of the good ideas came from them. They worked as a team, and we all took satisfaction in making a difference." He smiled. "Those were great times at Amtrak. And we sure had a lot of fun!"

Amtrak signs Operation
Redblock agreement with the
first 2 partner organizations

Perestroika begins
in the Soviet Union
January 1

Pan Am Flight 103
bombing occurs over
Lockerbie, Scotland
February 16

New or refurbished stations
open in Salt Lake City, Hartford,
Raleigh, and Martinez

Nonstop *Metroliner Service* is introduced
between Washington and New York and
features complimentary newspapers

Ticket sales from travel agencies
increase by nearly 20 percent

Amtrak's F40PH locomotives proved to be reliable for many years,
racking up millions of miles over their lifetime. The eastbound *Empire
Builder* is seen here in 1986 taking on fuel at Havre, Mont.

Thomas J. Van Haag

This collection of promotional brochures depicts various sales and marketing programs of the 1980s.

Railfone service installed on *San Diegans*, and service (one daily train) extends to Santa Barbara

Special 20th anniversary *Metroliner Service* trip takes place for media
January 12

First computerized yield management system is used to manage ticket sales

Restored Washington Union Station reopens in September to great fanfare

Superliner enhancements (movies, special menus, and other amenities) placed on the *Texas Eagle* and *Sunset Limited* complete the system-wide program

Amtrak President W. Graham Claytor Jr. led one of Amtrak's highlight efforts of the 1980s when the railroad was able to return to a newly restored Washington Union Station in September 1988.

Amtrak photo, Ann Owens collection

Carol M. Highsmith

The Main Hall was converted to a visitor's center for the Bicentennial. This area was known as "the pit" and featured screens with a slide show of the area's landmarks.

John Carten collection

Union Station was redeveloped, commercial venues were added to help ensure the vitality of the station going forward, and the décor was restored to its original beauty.

Revenue on Northeast Corridor trains grows more than 15 percent after move into restored Washington Union Station

For the second consecutive year, Amtrak carries more passengers between Washington and New York than all airlines combined

Montrealer service is reinstated after 2-year hiatus caused by deteriorating track in Vermont

Morning and afternoon nonstop *Metroliner Service* is added

104 privately financed Horizon cars, first short-distance cars acquired since 1977, are purchased

June 4
Tiananmen Square massacre takes place in China

With renewed focus on service, china and linen tablecloths return on the *Capitol Limited* and *Coast Starlight*

With sponsorship from Harrah's casino, service begins to Atlantic City

December 3
George Bush and Mikhail Gorbachev jointly announce that the Cold War is ending

Amtrak's eastbound *Broadway Limited*, Train 40, descends the famous Horseshoe Curve just west of Altoona, Pa.

1980s				
Fiscal Year	**Ridership**	**Stations Served**	**Passenger Miles (Millions)**	**Revenue (Millions)**
1980	21,219,149	525	4,582	428.7
1981	20,609,944	525	4,762	612.2
1982	19,042,325	506	4,172	630.7
1983	19,038,563	497	4,246	664.4
1984	19,943,075	510	4,552	758.8
1985	20,776,091	503	4,825	825.8
1986	20,327,909	491	5,012	861.4
1987	20,414,714	487	5,221	847
1988	21,496,303	498	5,678	947
1989	21,363,151	504	5,859	1,072

The useful life of Amtrak's Heritage fleet was extended when cars were converted from steam heat to an electrical head-end system. Here, passengers enjoy a meal in a converted Heritage dining car.

In 1989, Amtrak began taking delivery of new Horizon cars based on a commuter car design. The cars were the first in Amtrak's history purchased with private funding instead of federal money, reflecting positively on the confidence of the private sector in Amtrak's future.

As Amtrak moved into the 1990s, more changes were in store. The second generation of Amtrak's diesel locomotives would be coming online as well as new Superliner II and Viewliner cars which replaced the Heritage coaches and sleepers that served Amtrak well for so many years. In this photo, the *California Zephyr* travels across the Colorado River with two new P42 locomotives and Superliner II cars.

Challenging Times

EVERY DAY BEGAN THE SAME. At 7 a.m. Eastern time, the team would run through the list of people on the line:

Transportation? Here. System Ops? Here. Engineering? Here. Mechanical? Here. Passenger Services? Here.

In the early 1990s, with Amtrak still under the watch of W. Graham Claytor Jr., the top priority of the company was to improve operating and safety performance. So each day began with a number of executives and managers representing every division nationwide and all facets of the company on a conference call to address any operating issues from the day before and make sure everything was squared away for the morning rush hour. The emphasis was on accountability.

Lee Bullock

Nothing illustrated the way Amtrak was run better than that half-hour call. The company was still run very much as a traditional railroad—lots of involvement by senior management in day-to-day operations. Top-down management and decision-making. Vertical departments were operated centrally and independent of each other. But during that call they came together. The trains had to move. On-time performance was critical.

As the decade progressed, those at the top of the company began to reevaluate this traditional style of railroad management. They were moving people, not cargo. The system at the time sometimes resulted in a lack of coordination in field operations and service delivery as well as poor employee communications.

Gil Mallery

Delivering better service for passengers became more of a concern. Unfortunately, it was hard to do. Despite efforts to improve communications with employees and being more accessible by riding trains and visiting work sites, management could not get out from under the weight of constant political struggles and budget battles.

The funding problems that plagued Amtrak throughout its life were still very much present, even though Congress viewed Claytor as a respected and credible leader. There was always pressure for more efficiency in every area. That meant less attention on actually building a company.

When Claytor left Amtrak in 1993 after a 12-year term as president and CEO, the overwhelming sentiment was shock. Everyone knew he wouldn't stay forever, but it was such a transformative event, employees weren't sure what would come next. In many ways, Claytor was the ideal leader for Amtrak.

Thomas Downs succeeded Claytor, bringing with him a significantly different vision for the company. Downs didn't come from the railroad industry, which raised some questions among the team he came to lead. They wondered if things would change. Downs soon made up his mind that Amtrak needed to be reinvented as a customer-oriented transportation provider with a focus on improving its bottom line.

Claytor had done an enormous amount of work to give Amtrak railroading credibility, which it sorely needed. But now, the passenger became the priority.

To accomplish his overhaul, Downs led Amtrak through the most significant reorganization in its history. A popular trend at many big companies during that time was decentralization, and Downs believed that was the right answer for Amtrak too. Decision-making and accountability, he said, should be pushed out into the company and closer to the customer.

Strategic Business Units—SBUs as they were called—became the critical organizational feature in this new Amtrak. The company was divided into three SBUs based on geography and service type. Each had its own president, based in Philadelphia, Chicago, and Los Angeles. The corporate headquarters staff was reduced to handle only necessary business functions.

Naturally, reactions among employees were mixed. Could this be the magic bullet for Amtrak or would it be the death blow to an unstable company? Those in the field were excited about their new influence. The Operations group was skeptical. This was a railroad, they thought, and a railroad is about moving trains as efficiently as possible. Centralized operating control was always the most important.

Creating the SBUs would give local management the power and responsibility to take care of customers.

On paper, the reorganization seemed like a good idea. Many states had invested heavily in passenger rail development, and they were frustrated by a perceived lack of ability to respond quickly and effectively to their needs. They felt that everything had to go through headquarters, which was slow and arduous.

As the reorganization started to shake out, excitement grew. Employees felt more empowered and tried new ideas. States wanted new partnerships and upped their investments in equipment and infrastructure improvements.

Amtrak bid on, and won, additional contracts to operate and support various commuter train services across the country. Winning these contracts reflected well on Amtrak's expertise in railroad operations. The bottom line of the company improved somewhat as a result of these contracts.

This period also included a radical expansion of mail and express services—a cause for controversy and tension with freight railroads and many employees. Operating a large number of freight cars on the passenger trains sometimes interfered with the mission of Amtrak as a subsidized passenger railroad. Some freight carriers were quick to voice their opinion that Amtrak had no right to this kind of business. This initiative did not last long enough to clearly demonstrate its ability to improve the bottom line.

There remained questions about whether it had any positive financial impact at all. It did, however, demonstrate the company's ability to meet challenges formerly considered insurmountable. Employees, both management and union, came up with creative solutions that indeed were often stunning.

Amtrak also experimented, much more successfully, in a field that was more clearly within its charter as the nation's passenger railroad: high-speed rail. Since the earliest days of the Northeast Corridor, it had been clear to Amtrak and its supporters that the Corridor was a resource whose potential was not fully exploited. During the Claytor administration, the Northeast Corridor Improvement Project had made a program of limited, but deftly directed, investment that allowed Amtrak to improve the reliability and top speed of its trains—and Amtrak's market share grew accordingly. Plans grew to extend electrification and high-speed service all the way up New England to Boston, and Amtrak experimented with foreign high-speed trains. It was left to Downs and the board of directors in 1996 to formally initiate the procurement program that would give Amtrak the service that has become its signature—*Acela Express*. Even as financial challenges loomed, he encouraged and sustained the program, never losing faith in its promise or its potential. Today, *Acela* is the company's largest revenue generator and was a key driver in Amtrak capturing the larger percentage of the Northeast Corridor air/rail traffic.

As the decade progressed, Amtrak's financial challenges became more difficult. The Clinton administration tilted in a friendlier direction to Amtrak than its predecessors and truly wanted to see it succeed. However, funding for new equipment, for state-of-the-art maintenance on the Northeast Corridor, and for aging and deteriorated facilities and stations was inadequate. The Clinton administration was facing huge financial challenges of its own, related mostly to its efforts to balance the federal budget. That did not give them the leeway to invest more heavily in passenger rail.

Without realizing the complete development of his vision of change, Downs left his post in 1998. George Warrington then became acting president and CEO for the company, and the board of directors subsequently awarded him the permanent job.

The decade of the 1990s was one of profound upheaval at Amtrak and fundamental change, perhaps more than any other decade: a significant statement for a company in constant turmoil.

Lee Bullock held various positions at Amtrak from 1973 to 2002 including assistant general superintendent in Chicago, superintendent of MBTA Commuter Service, vice president of Customer Service for Amtrak West, president of Amtrak Intercity Strategic Business Unit, and vice president for Freight Railroad Relations. He is now retired.

Gil Mallery was president of Amtrak West Strategic Business Unit and served as vice president for Planning and Business Development. Currently, he is part of the high-speed rail team at an engineering firm.

58 Horizon cars
are delivered
to Amtrak

Conference Club Car is
put into regular service on
Metroliner Service trains

Amtrak adds 5 state-supported services:
2 *Hiawatha* frequencies, the *Gulf Breeze*, the
Carolinian, and an additional *San Joaquin* train

Amtrak's Metropolitan Lounge opens in New
York for first class sleeping car and Club Service
passengers, the first of several such lounges

July 26
President Bush signs the
Americans with Disabilities Act

1991

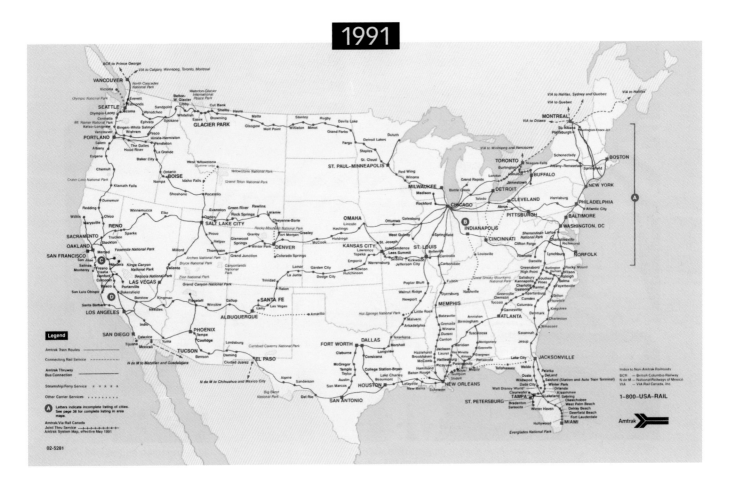

As part of an experiment, former *Metroliner* Snack Coach 863 was converted into an conference cab car, numbered 9800, for use in *Metroliner Service*. The car had five onboard conference rooms and became popular with business travelers.

Amtrak photo, Ann Owens collection

Conductor Carolyn Price operates a hand-thrown switch, so her train goes down the right track.

Doug Riddell

Automatic Train Control installation
is completed on all locomotives
operating on the Northeast Corridor

Operation Desert Storm begins;
it ends on February 28
January 16

New 3 hour 55 minute express
service is developed between
Boston and New York

First class dining facilities
are added to the *Auto Train*

October 3
Germany is formally reunified

Amtrak's Metropolitan Lounges
open in Chicago and Washington

Keystone Classic Club is introduced
on Philadelphia-Pittsburgh service;
it runs through June 28, 1992

Amtrak photo, Ann Owens collection

The last dome diners in regular service were on Amtrak's *Auto Train*. In the 1990s, this too would come to an end as the delivery of Superliner II equipment replaced the last of the Heritage equipment on the *Auto Train*.

John Carten collection

Going into 1990, Southampton Yard in Boston received its first indoor service and inspection building. For the first time, mechanical employees did not have to fix railcars outside in the snow and rain. An F40 locomotive sits on the east end of the shop next to the new facility.

Dave Warner

As traffic congestion worsened in the Bay Area, the state of California and Amtrak partnered to launch a new corridor service between San Jose and Sacramento called the Capitol Corridor.

Travel agency sales account for about 40 percent of Amtrak ticket sales

After a brief coup, the Soviet Union collapses, and republics declare independence in following week
August 19

Congress votes to fund additional improvements between New York and Boston

June 14-16
Philadelphia 30th Street Station is rededicated after a major renovation

Empire tunnel connection is completed in New York, linking New York Penn Station with Metro-North line, which runs upstate

Amtrak begins operating Virginia Railway Express commuter rail service

On April 4, 1991, W. Graham Claytor Jr. gave a speech to celebrate Amtrak moving the last intercity rail service from Grand Central Terminal to New York Penn Station.

From left, Robert E. Gall, vice president Sales, Neil D. Mann, assistant vice president Personnel, Anthony D. DeAngelo, vice president Real Estate and Operations Development, and Timothy P. Gardner, vice president Passenger Marketing enjoy the celebration on the first TurboTrain to operate from Albany to Penn Station.

A train climbs the famous Cuesta Grade north of San Luis Obispo, Calif., on the route of the *Coast Starlight*.

Capitol Corridor trains complete first full month in California (3 daily round trips)

For the first time, Amtrak carries more commuter passengers than intercity passengers

$32 million renovation of Chicago Union Station and facilities is completed by Metra and Amtrak

20 P32-8BWH locomotives are delivered, first of the new generation of GE-built engines

May 22
Johnny Carson retires from the *Tonight Show* after 30 years and is replaced by Jay Leno

Phil Gosney

Amtrak Train 715 heads towards the afternoon sun at Pinole, Calif., on its way from Bakersfield to Oakland on June 23, 1995. Engine 508 is one of 20 P32-8BWH locomotives purchased in 1991 from GE.

Amtrak photo, Ann Owens collection

The panoramic view from the many large windows on a Superliner Sightseer Lounge always attracts a crowd no matter what train it's on.

Amtrak photo, Ann Owens collection

As the original Superliners entered their second decade of service, they were painted in the Phase III paint scheme with red, white, and blue stripes.

Amtrak's Metropolitan Lounge opens at Philadelphia 30th Street Station

World Trade Center in New York City is bombed
February 26

22 P40 locomotives are delivered and put into service

November 3
Bill Clinton is elected 42nd president of the United States

Amtrak receives 5th annual Harriman Award for safety

Amtrak begins testing of German ICE and Swedish X2000 trains on the Northeast Corridor

Doug Riddell

In 1993, Amtrak hosted two foreign high-speed guests to test the latest in high-speed rail technology. Here, the Swedish X2000 arrives at Washington Terminal.

Julie Byrne collection

The X2000 featured a modern, European-styled Bistro car. Lead Service Attendant Julie Byrne enjoys serving passengers in this high-speed café.

Ira Silverman

On March 31, 1993, a special inaugural train was operated to celebrate the extension of the *Sunset Limited* from New Orleans to Miami. The special is seen pausing at Gulfport, Miss., while being well received by the city.

Linda Anderson: Working on a Bet

In 1994, she had been working as a paralegal with a construction company in Washington, D.C., on a temporary basis. During a downtown jaunt with a friend, she saw an advertisement for an opening—all they had to do was take a quick entrance exam. "My girlfriend said, 'We're downtown, let's take the test. I bet you won't,'" she remembers. "I told her we'd only do it for the summer." Her friend didn't make the cut. But Linda did. "That summer turned into 16 years for me."

Already 41, Anderson wasn't anticipating a major career change. But suddenly she found herself working as a train attendant on board the *Capitol Limited*, running between Chicago and Washington. She worked the coaches, the sleeper, and the diner, and before long was promoted to the lead service attendant position.

"I really thoroughly enjoyed the train; it was very refreshing," she says. "I liked the people. It was never the same trip twice. You're always going to meet someone new or have some exciting adventure. Some other times you're going to meet someone rough around the edges. That's life."

The semi-itinerant lifestyle was nothing new to Anderson. The child of an Air Force officer, she was used to moving around: "I grew up everywhere, all over Europe," she says. She didn't even live in the United States before her junior year in high school. "I grew up a traveler."

In April 1995, Anderson was furloughed…for two whole weeks. She rejoined the company on the *Auto Train*, offering premier service from the East Coast of Virginia to Florida. She was the first to interview for the job, and she was the first to get it. "I was very fortunate," she says. "When it's your destiny, it's your destiny."

That destiny took her to New Orleans, where she worked the *Crescent* and *City of New Orleans* routes. Then, in 1997, she became a union supervisor for six years—her first taste of management—before being briefly furloughed again. She returned to Washington and worked on trains again. In 2002, she transferred to Miami and then came back to Washington. Finally, in 2006, she was promoted to manager of onboard services, where she has been ever since.

Anderson's military upbringing has served her well, managing onboard services for the *Capitol Limited*. (Ms. Anderson is sometimes referred to as the Drill Sergeant.) She is responsible for the passenger services crew, with a large staff under her on an overnight train that runs seven days a week in both directions. The shift is three days on and three days off—a total of 31 to 35 hours a trip. Her staff is entitled to four hours of downtime, either between 10 p.m. and 2 a.m. or 2 a.m. and 6 a.m. "It's a tough job," says Anderson. "It's not for everyone. Uniforms must be cleaned and pressed. Our shirts are white, not beige. Our crews take great pride in their professional appearance and always try to present that look on the platform as they welcome their passengers aboard the *Capitol Limited* or the *Cardinal*."

And if they miss the mark by chance? "We do have an iron at the crew base," she says with a chuckle. Her attention to detail serves her—and her crews—well.

Every now and then, company CEO Joe Boardman latches his car onto the *Capitol Limited*. "I've had the privilege of riding with him," says Anderson. "It's always enjoyable. Mr. Boardman is very down to earth, hardworking, very sincere, and dedicated. He sets the example. He uses our product, and he gives us an overview of what he sees. I think he's got us on the right track, no pun intended."

Anderson has her staff on the right track as well. In 2007, a few months after starting her position, there were four or five injuries on her route, she says. The following year, the record improved greatly. The safety briefings and incorporation of Safe2Safer into our program with the understanding that we are our brothers' and sisters' keeper has made a difference to the crews, Anderson says. "They are more informed and aware. It helped really teach us that seven people come together and work a train as one—whether coaches, sleeper, diner, or whatever. In the end, we're going to make this trip as a unit of seven people, and we're going to make sure the customers get what they need and get home safely."

Linda has no intention of deviating from her current mission. She says her next move, she hopes, will be to progress to the next level of management in her division. "It's not for everybody," she says. "You have to have patience, compassion, and a special place for people." And a flair for adventure. It would be unwise to bet against her.

Amtrak places Viewliner order and ultimately receives 50 sleeping cars

Procurement process begins for an order of 26 high-speed trainsets

Amtrak's worst accident occurs after barge damages Big Bayou Canot bridge and *Sunset Limited* derails; 47 people die and 103 are injured

September 22

Amtrak attains 43 percent share of air-rail market between Washington and New York

New Reservation Sales Office is completed at Riverside, Calif., with 400 modern work stations

Sunset Limited extends east to Miami

The German-built Intercity Express (ICE) train, the second high-speed foreign guest, passes over the Peck Moveable Drawbridge in Bridgeport, Conn., on its way to New Haven.

Lead Service Attendant Justin Collins prepares to serve food on board the ICE train's modern and high-ceilinged Bistro car.

At the conclusion of its American tour, Amtrak would say auf Wiedersehen to the ICE train. It would be taken to Baltimore, loaded on a ship, and returned to its homeland.

South Africa holds its
first multiracial elections,
officially ending apartheid
April 27

Montrealer and *River Cities*
services are discontinued

Operation of leased Talgo trains begins
in partnership with Washington State
Department of Transportation

First phase of modernization of
New York Penn Station Control
Center is completed

Amtrak photo, Blair Slaughter collection

In 1993, Amtrak began taking delivery of a second generation of Superliner cars, including this dining car photographed at the Bombardier assembly plant in Barre, Vt. The first generation of Superliners came from Pullman-Standard in Chicago.

Amtrak photo, John Carten collection

The Amtrak facility in Wilmington, Del., cares for all the electric locomotives, including AEM-7 no. 902, hoisted into the air above its wheels and suspension (trucks).

Blair Slaughter collection

This photo shows the interior of a brand new Superliner II sleeper roomette.

Amtrak photo, Ann Owens collection

Operating in the 1990s on the same tracks it had traveled for more than 30 years is a former Santa Fe Railway hi-level railcar, with its distinctive zigzag stripe, coupled to a series of Amtrak Superliners on the *Southwest Limited* between Chicago and Los Angeles. The Santa Fe cars inspired the Superliners design.

8 states increase financial support
for Amtrak partnerships

Major service reductions
cut train miles by 16 percent

November 13
First passengers travel through
undersea Channel Tunnel that
links England and France

3 Strategic Business Units are formed: Northeast
Corridor, Intercity, and West; streamlined corporate
headquarters remains in Washington, D.C.

North Carolina inaugurates state-
supported *Piedmont* service

Mike Schafer

In 1993 at Joliet, Ill., the *Ann Rutledge* takes on passengers before traveling to Abraham Lincoln's hometown of Springfield, Ill., and then on to St. Louis and Kansas City. The *Rutledge* was named by a predecessor railroad for a young woman thought at the time to be Lincoln's first love, which present-day scholars now dispute.

Doug Riddell collection

Deborah Kelly-Chaison is at the controls of P40 locomotive 811 on the head end of the *Pennsylvanian* at a time when female engineers were less common than today.

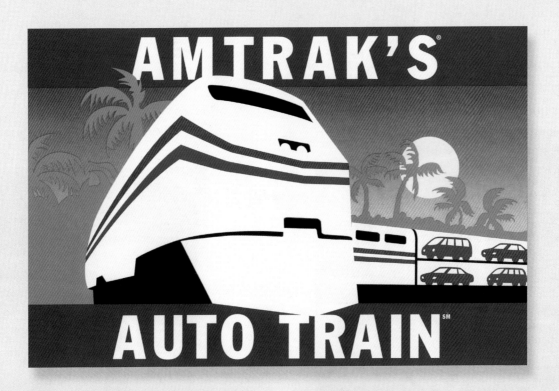

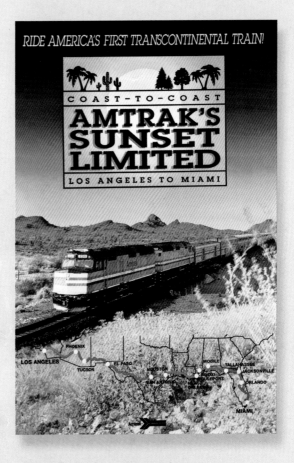

Known now as the *Acela Express*, the newest generation of high-speed trains was once going to carry the name of a model train best known by previous generations. In the 1990s, Amtrak offered passengers a variety of services: the *Auto Train*, which carried passengers and their vehicles from Lorton, Va., to Sanford, Fla.; the *Sunset Limited*, which in 1993 began operating from Los Angeles to Miami, an experiment that ended in 1996; and daily service in winter to locations that featured nearby ski resorts.

Vermonter service is introduced in partnership with the state of Vermont

Broadway Limited is discontinued and replaced by *Three Rivers*; East Coast-Midwest service is restructured

eBay is founded
September 4

Amfleet I cars are upgraded with amenities such as 110V electric power for early laptop computers and accessible restrooms

Palmetto frequencies are reduced and *Gulf Breeze* discontinued due to budget cuts

November 28
The federal 55 mph automobile speed limit ends

Amtrak photo, John Carten collection

Passengers count on Amtrak in all seasons, but few times are more challenging than coupling cars and locomotives on this winter day in the Washington, D.C., terminal.

Sam Caliciotti

On his way to the Democratic National Convention in Chicago in 1996 and his nomination for a second term, President Bill Clinton chartered an Amtrak train and posed in the door of a *Metroliner* with a hat borrowed from an Amtrak conductor.

Amtrak photo, Ann Owens collection

In the 1990s, as part of a plan to improve the quality of food service, Amtrak sent its chefs to the Culinary Institute of America. Here, a chef aboard a Superliner prepares breakfast on a flattop grill.

During a paralyzing blizzard, Amtrak maintains service on the Northeast Corridor, the only intercity mode to do so
January 7

Delivery of 36 Viewliner cars, the first single-level sleepers manufactured in 40 years

$2 million is donated to inaugurate the Great American Station Foundation to help communities repair and improve their train stations

Dolly the sheep, the first animal to be successfully cloned, is born
July 5

Groundbreaking ceremony takes place for North End electrification, which allows higher speeds between New Haven and Boston

Amtrak announces that computer systems will be made Y2K-compliant

Amtrak introduces CPR and first aid training for crew members as part of annual emergency training curriculum

For the first time, an Amtrak service covers its operating costs as *Metroliner Service* generates $14 million

Tunnels between Baltimore and Boston are too short to accommodate Amtrak Superliner sleeping cars, so Amtrak purchased 50 Viewliner sleeping cars to replace 40-year-old sleeping cars passed down from predecessors.

Women filled more roles on the railroad in this decade, from locomotive engineers to those who give them orders. Pictured here are mother and daughter, Anne Clausen and Carrie Guion.

Popular for two rows of windows in each room, Viewliner sleeping car deliveries took place in 1995-1996.

Amtrak relaunched the *Coast Starlight* in 1995 with exclusive service and amenities just for sleeping car passengers aboard the Pacific Parlour Car, where Eliseo Nora is seen displaying a platter served during a wine and cheese tasting. Such upgrades increased ridership, and financial performance improved.

75

Paula Porter: A Train Enthusiast

When Paula Porter arrived at Amtrak in 1995, the first thing that struck her was the employees' intense dedication to the place. "They're train fanatics," she says, and their enthusiasm is catching. "Many of them are second, third, and fourth generation railroaders, and they're very connected to the product. You don't see that in banking!"

Banking had been Paula's sphere for more than 25 years. She grew up in Dayton, Ohio, the oldest of eight children raised by a single mother in tough circumstances. Paula went to work for Bank of America as a work measurement analyst where, over the years, she held increasingly responsible positions, first in Ohio and then in Washington, D.C. Ultimately, she become disenchanted with the turbulence and change in financial services, especially with the continuous mergers and acquisitions and deals of the late 1980s and early 1990s. So she left and took a few months to think about her future. "I decided that I needed a new challenge, an opportunity to truly make a difference, and I found a new home with Amtrak. I responded to a blind ad for a leadership development director, which had always been my passion. Those of us who have been in Human Resources for a while know it's challenging to get anything through a blind ad, but Amtrak called me back! The job was in Corporate Leadership Development, and it captured my interest."

In those days, Amtrak had three Strategic Business Units reporting into the corporate umbrella in Washington, D.C., and Paula was responsible for coordinating leadership development for the entire company. She felt at home immediately. She realized that she could immediately make a difference. "I had a connection with, and respect for, what we were doing. And everyone understood that this was a national railroad system and the primary stakeholders were the American public, the federal government, and the president of the United States."

As she describes it, "Everyone may not agree on policy and procedure, but it's the only company I know where all employees are unanimous in their passion for the product (trains). You can go into anyone's work area and see railroad paraphernalia of some sort. When I first arrived, people would comment that I had nothing in my office that related to trains or the railroad." Fortunately, she found a suitable item in a pile of trash, a set of three tattered prints depicting antique locomotives in scenic landscapes. She hung them on the wall and that settled things—they have been her pride and joy ever since.

Learning the culture of Amtrak also meant learning the lingo. Paula laughs as she recounts an early misunderstanding on her first long-distance train trip a month or so into the job. She was going to Chicago, leaving in the afternoon and arriving the following morning. "I had never slept on a train or been in a sleeping car, and I noticed during the night that we were stopped for an unusual amount of time. So I grabbed my robe and slippers and went out to investigate. I found an attendant who let me know that the "crew had died." I said, 'What happened? What's going on? Did you call the police?' I think I'm going to lose my mind; I have tears in my eyes. And this guy is look-

ing at me wondering why I'm so upset and I'm wondering why he's not." It turned out that "died" meant that the crew had taken a mandatory rest break. Not long afterwards, Paula had a group of people involved in training put together a dictionary of railroad terms for new hires.

For the last 10 years, Paula has worked as assistant vice president of Human Resources, responsible for recruitment, planning, training, and career counseling, human resources policy administration, and talent management. Like her colleagues, she's learned that accommodating and effectuating change is a big part of the job. Each new president brings in new ideas and people—and a different management style. So with each new president, there also came new opportunities to strengthen relationships and become a stronger Amtrak family.

And speaking of family, at 6 a.m. one recent Saturday, Paula went to volunteer alongside an Amtrak colleague who was assembling and delivering food packages to needy families for Thanksgiving as part of a Project Give Back initiative. It made her very happy to do so, partly because it was an employee's project, but also because her family had received help from similar groups when she was a child. "This effort is near and dear to my heart," she says now. "If it had not been for this type of organization, my family probably would have had more of a struggle. It's not easy being a single mom of eight in a Rust Belt town. I'm proud of my mother, and she's proud of me. And all of us kids are just fine, doing our own thing."

Paula plans to be working at Amtrak for several more years but says when she retires she'll surely be riding the trains. Her favorite route is the trip between Oakland and Los Angeles. "Riding along the ocean when the sun is just coming up is absolutely gorgeous! I also love the mountains of Virginia and West Virginia when you're going from Chicago to Washington. And the route to Boston is nice because of the water and the mountains…I guess I'm an enthusiast!" It's not exactly a surprise to hear that Paula now has a model diesel engine on display in her home office. "Who would ever have thought it would be possible?" she says, laughing, "coming from the inner city in Dayton, Ohio, where I never saw a train!"

Amtrak photo, Ann Owens collection

Under New York City law, trains must use electric power to and from Penn Station, so special dual-mode locomotives, such as Amtrak 705, are able to pick up electrical power from a "shoe" that contacts a third rail on the route to Albany-Rensselaer.

Amtrak photo, Blair Slaughter collection

Amtrak 486 was built for the old New Haven Railroad and operated for more than 40 years before Amtrak 705 (above) was delivered by GE in 1995.

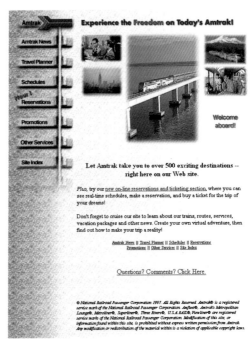

In 1997, the Amtrak home on the World Wide Web could show you where the trains were going and was just beginning the now-common functionality of accepting reservations and selling tickets.

Red River floods and inundates parts of Minnesota and North Dakota
April 18

Great American Station Foundation whistle-stop tour welcomes more than 50,000 visitors to view railroad station history

Metroliner Service sets a ridership record

Special self-contained ventilated smoking rooms are introduced on 59 long-distance cars

Amtrak has 11 state partners

Ivy City yard is cleared for construction of high-speed rail maintenance facility in preparation for *Acela Express*

In 1993, Amtrak's first true transcontinental was begun when the Los Angeles-New Orleans *Sunset Limited* was extended east to Miami. In this 1995 photo, a Superliner-equipped train heads east over the Escambia Bay just outside of Pensacola, Fla., on the new route.

Amtrak photo

Train 5, the *California Zephyr*, is just out of Denver on the second day of its trip to California and is just beginning its assault on the Front Range of the Rocky Mountains.

Passenger revenue passes
$1 billion for the first time in
Amtrak's history

Amtrak partners with 9 states
to propose the Midwest
Regional Rail Initiative

Consolidated National Operations
Center opens in Wilmington, Del.

Talgo trainsets debut
on *Cascades* service

Company launches Res2000 to improve
station ticketing, reservations, customer
information, and accounting functions

Seattle, Centralia, Salem,
and Sacramento stations
are renovated

Amtrak photo, Ann Owens collection

Matt Donnelly

Old meets new—41 years separate these two locomotives. The new F59PHI, ordered for *Surfliner* service, was delivered to the Rensselaer maintenance facility in 1998 before being shipped west. Here, it is coupled to one of Amtrak's oldest active road diesels, FL9 485.

George Pitz

Although it was delivered with direct current (DC) technology and Phase III stripes, locomotive 905 has been converted to an alternating current (AC) system and wears Phase IV striping for use in *Northeast-Direct* service.

Amtrak photo

Family travel has been at the heart of passenger trains since the earliest days. This family is boarding the east-bound *Southwest Chief* on its Los Angeles-Chicago route.

Amtrak's Air-Rail Travel Plan '94

TWO GREAT WAYS TO TRAVEL ONE GREAT PRICE

AMTRAK

THERE'S SOMETHING ABOUT A TRAIN THAT'S MAGIC.

Call Aboard!

Railfone
GTE

SIEMENS   AEG

ICE Train:
The Hottest
Thing on Rails

ADIRONDACK
TRAVEL GUIDE

X2000
DEMONSTRATION

High Speed Rail for America!

ABB

CRESCENT

Crescent
New York ★ Washington, DC
Atlanta ★ New Orleans

Gulf Breeze
New York ★ Washington, DC
Atlanta ★ Birmingham ★ Mobile

ROUTE GUIDE

SUMMER FARES

Auto Train
Summer
Forecast:
Hot
Fares,
Cool
Savings

WASHINGTON—FLORIDA

All Aboard Michigan!

A TRAVELER'S GUIDE TO
MICHIGAN'S RAIL
PASSENGER SERVICE

AMTRAK

CARDINAL

ROUTE GUIDE
★ Chicago ★ Indianapolis
★ Cincinnati ★ Washington, D.C.

CASCADES

A NEW TRAIN
FOR A NEW ERA

ACTIVITY GUIDE

Silver Service
AMTRAK

DISCOVER COUNTLESS ADVENTURES

Superior Service
Superior Food Superior Fun
The Renaissance of The
COAST STARLIGHT

Amtrak's Hottest Train
With the Coolest Scenery

AMTRAK'S METROPOLITAN LOUNGE

Chicago's Premier
Point of Arrival
and Departure
for the
First Class
Traveler

Amtrak®
International
Chicago-Toronto

Serving Niles, Kalamazoo, Battle Creek,
East Lansing, Durand, Flint, Lapeer,
Port Huron and Canadian destinations!

Michigan

AMTRAK'S
KEYSTONE
CLASSIC CLUB

LUXURY DAYTIME SERVICE
BETWEEN NEW YORK AND PITTSBURGH

Amtrak has racks of literature at many stations to promote new services and features, giving everyone a chance to plan another trip or catch a glimpse of a route. The route guides are also distributed aboard many trains, providing passengers with information about the history and the

AMTRAK

COMMUTER RAIL SERVICES

Moving People by Rail is Our Business!

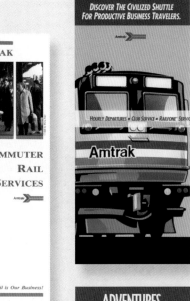

DISCOVER THE CIVILIZED SHUTTLE FOR PRODUCTIVE BUSINESS TRAVELERS.

Hourly Departures • Club Service • Railfone™ Service

Amtrak

WELCOME ABOARD

Amtrak's Montrealer

AMTRAK

THE THREE Rivers

ROUTE GUIDE

Chicago ★ Pittsburgh
Philadelphia ★ New York

NORTHEAST DIRECT

RICHMOND & WILLIAMSBURG

"Take the train to Virginia and see what we have to offer!"

PIONEER

Follow The Oregon Trail

ADVENTURES AWAIT ON THE LAKE SHORE LIMITED.

AMTRAK LAKE SHORE LIMITED
NEW YORK • BOSTON • CHICAGO

Fall/Winter 1998-1999 Activity Guide

SOUTHWEST CHIEF

Chicago ★ Kansas City ★ Albuquerque
Flagstaff ★ Los Angeles

ROUTE Amtrak GUIDE

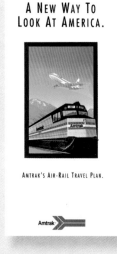

INTRODUCING A NEW WAY TO LOOK AT AMERICA.

Amtrak's Air-Rail Travel Plan.

SKI AMTRAK

1990 · 1991

Amtrak's Auto Train
Between Florida and the Northeast

FAMILIES FARE BETTER WITH SPECIAL SUMMER RATES

KIDS 2-15 TRAVEL FOR $29 One-Way With An Adult

Summer 1994
June 17–Sept. 30, 1994

AMTRAK

TEXAS EAGLE

ROUTE GUIDE

★ Chicago ★ St. Louis
★ Dallas/Forth Worth
★ San Antonio/Houston

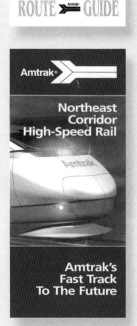

Amtrak

Northeast Corridor High-Speed Rail

Amtrak's Fast Track To The Future

Amtrak's USA RAIL PASS

EXPERIMENTE LA VASTA Y SORPRENDENTE BELLEZA DE LOS ESTADOS UNIDOS, CON LA COMODIDAD Y EL ESTILO DE AMTRAK.

AMTRAK
HAY ALGO MÁGICO SOBRE LOS TRENES

Amtrak

Amtrak's VERMONTER

TRAVEL GUIDE

Travel through Vermont on Amtrak's Vermonter!

Follow the scenic route inside

sights along the way. Among those shown here are for the Railfone, an early cellular technology, and the Air-Rail program, which enabled return trips by air before the Internet turned many travelers into their own travel planners.

Google is founded
September 4

December 2
Exxon and Mobil merge
to create the world's
largest corporation

1999

Amtrak Train 59 and a truck
collide at Bourbonnais, Ill.
(11 dead, 122 injured)
March 15

March 29
Dow Jones Industrial
Average closes above
10,000 for the first time

1990s

Fiscal Year	Ridership	Stations Served	Passenger Miles (Millions)	Revenue (Millions)
1990	22,186,300	516	5,330	878
1991	22,062,425	523	5,304	908
1992	21,345,247	524	5,166	872
1993	22,065,869	535	5,050	885
1994	21,837,626	540	5,545	827
1995	20,726,490	530	5,921	827
1996	19,605,398	542	6,199	850
1997	20,190,450	516	6,091	916
1998	21,094,165	508	6,273	946
1999	21,508,694	510	6,057	1,003

Amtrak photo

Amtrak advanced automatic-vending technology in this decade with large self-service Quik-Trak ticketing machines. These first-generation Quik-Traks, lined up at Washington Union Station, each weighed 600 pounds and were in service from 1993 to 2006.

John Carten

The Claytor Concourse at Washington Union Station is always busy, but never more so than during the Thanksgiving holiday travel season, as captured here.

Amtrak photo, John Carten collection

The crews who maintain tracks and ties, or as seen here replacing a bridge, are unsung heroes of the railroad, working overnight and unseen by most passengers.

After a 20-year absence, passenger
service in Oklahoma is reintroduced
with the *Heartland Flyer*

June 15

First rebuilt Amfleet cars emerge from Capstone
program designed to enhance comfort and
comply with Americans with Disabilities Act

Amtrak declares its computer
systems Y2K compliant

Travis Pratt

As part of the Northeast High Speed Rail Improvement Project, construction began in the 1990s to extend catenary wires from New Haven to Boston that would allow electric service to begin at the start of the next decade.

Amtrak photo

Soldiering on into the 1990s and beyond were dining cars older than many of their passengers. Amtrak modernized the interiors in some Heritage diners for yet another time in 1999. It will be another 10 years before Amtrak has the funds to order replacements.

Using the knowledge gained from overseas visits in the 1990s and U.S. tours of the X2000 and ICE trains, Amtrak worked with the consortium of Alstom and Bombardier to produce the fastest train in North America, the *Acela Express*, which operates at speeds up to 150 mph.

Gary Pancavage

America's Railroad

THE FIRST DECADE OF THE 21ST CENTURY
was one of opportunity, innovation, and challenge
for the company.

By 2000, on the positive side, Amtrak had completed the electrification and other upgrades of
the Washington-Boston corridor. The trainsets that
would be used for *Acela Express* service, the first
true high-speed train in the United States, were
just about ready to go into service. They would
be a valuable supplement to the Amfleet cars
and Superliner fleet, which were
proving to be tough and durable
equipment.

David Gunn

Later in the decade, Amtrak
began a $145 million improve-
ment program on the Harrisburg
Line in Pennsylvania. Completion
of that program in 2006 allowed
trains to operate at up to
110 mph between Harrisburg
and Philadelphia. The improve-
ments allowed for faster, more frequent service
and resulted in significant ridership growth. It was
a major achievement that illustrates the technical
skill and resourcefulness of the company.

On the negative side, there were significant
storm clouds on the horizon. The company
finances were in desperate shape. Years of trying
to force the company to be profitable or self-
sufficient had done serious damage.

There was massive deferral of plant and equipment maintenance. There were no heavy overhaul
programs for rolling stock. The fleet was tired and
looked it.

Amtrak-owned facilities were deteriorating.
Repairs were basically done as things failed. There
was no significant program to maintain, much less
upgrade, rail and track infrastructure.

But the deferral of maintenance did not stop
the slide toward insolvency. By the spring of 2002,
the company was running out of cash. Without
an infusion of money, Amtrak would not meet its
payroll in early summer.

The first major step to bring costs back under
control and create efficiencies was to abolish the
Strategic Business Units that had been in place
since the late 1990s and reinstitute a traditional
railroad structure with centralized operations.

In spite of the Bush administration, which was
not pro-rail, Amtrak was able to convince Congress to tide Amtrak over to the beginning of the
new fiscal year in October 2002.

Following that near-death experience, Amtrak management and the board of directors focused on five things.

First was regaining fiscal control and discipline, which included returning to generally accepted accounting principles and eliminating weaknesses in the financial system, as well as instituting strict head-count control. From 2001 to 2005, the number of employees was reduced from nearly 25,000 to just over 19,000.

Second on the list was developing and implementing a State of Good Repair capital program that focused on plant and equipment. There was a massive increase in track work. The company installed almost no concrete ties in fiscal year 2002, but installed a total of 416,000 over the next three years. Over that same time, 169,000 wood ties were also replaced. In fiscal year 2002, only eight miles of severely worn rail were replaced, but over the next three years, Amtrak replaced 341 miles of rail. Turnout replacement increased from 37 to 271 between 2003 and 2005.

Heavy repair programs for passenger rolling stock, diesel work locomotives and switch engines, and electric locomotives were undertaken at the mechanical facilities in Bear and Wilmington, Del., and Beech Grove, Ind. Those programs allowed Amtrak to overhaul 275 Amfleet cars, 96 Superliners, 29 Horizon cars, and 65 pieces of maintenance-of-way equipment during the early part of the decade. Another 60 cars that had damage were rebuilt to add much needed capacity.

Fiscal Year:	2002	2003	2004	2005
Concrete Ties Replaced	0	104,000	152,000	160,000
Wood Ties Replaced	16,000	49,000	59,000	45,000
Fencing Replaced (feet)	3,000	3,000	17,000	10,000
Rail Replaced (rail miles)	8	26	240	75
Turnouts Replaced	37	52	115	104
Heavy Overhauls				
Amfleet Cars	17	20	114	124
Superliners	0	0	39	57
MOW Equipment	0	0	31	34
Horizon Cars	0	0	1	28
Wrecks rebuilt	6	22	29	3

The third area of emphasis, which went hand-in-hand with the State of Good Repair program, was elevating the importance of material acquisition and storage by making it a direct-report to the president. Successfully completing all those infrastructure and equipment projects depended on an adequate flow of material so the company improved storage capability. A side benefit of this focus on materials was the identification of millions of dollars worth of scrap and reusable materials.

Fourth, the company developed a strategy for reducing the financial losses on long-haul trains. The strategy was exemplified by work on the *Empire Builder*—improved quality helped fill the train, allowing the price to be raised faster than costs.

And finally, Amtrak focused on making *Acela Express* work. There were significant teething problems when the service first began. At one point, every trainset had to be taken out of service because of a design failure in the disc brakes. This wasn't terribly surprising given the technological leap represented in the equipment.

The new, traditional organizational structure allowed Amtrak to overcome the setback and quickly cobble together replacement service using Amfleet equipment. It obviously affected trip times, but there was no significant loss of capacity during those few months until the high-speed trains were returned to service.

This issue exemplified the need to focus on the other four areas and showed how critical it is to coordinate procurement, materials management, and operations. To gain complete control over the service, *Acela Express* maintenance, which had been outsourced to the manufacturer, was brought in-house. Regaining control solved a number of problems. Demand for *Acela Express* was high and continued its strong growth.

Amazingly enough, it all worked. Head count dropped, production increased, the operating deficit slowly dropped, and market share on the Northeast Corridor grew significantly.

Despite some success, Amtrak's journey through the early 21st century was bumpy. The company had five presidents in 10 years: George Warrington (1998-2002), David Gunn (2002-2005), David Hughes (2006), Alex Kummant (2006-2008), and Joe Boardman (2008-present). Additionally, the board of directors completely turned over three times, making management inconsistent at best. Relationships with freight railroads were strained.

The good news is that upon closing out its first 40 years, Americans renewed their love of train travel. Amtrak's ridership grew by 37 percent during the decade, despite the biggest economic crash since the Great Depression. States were knocking on the door to get new services. The Obama administration was committed to developing passenger rail, which it illustrated by committing $8 billion in federal funds.

Selling the importance of rail transportation will be tough on Capitol Hill and on Main Street. The future may not be clear, but for Amtrak, it certainly has potential.

David Gunn was Amtrak's president and chief executive officer from 2002 to 2005. David previously was general manager and chief operating office of Southeastern Pennsylvania Transportation Authority (SEPTA), president of the New York City Transit Authority, general manager for the Washington Metropolitan Area Transit Authority (WMATA), and chief general manager of the Toronto Transit Commission. He is now retired and lives in Nova Scotia.

AOL announces an agreement to purchase Time-Warner in the largest corporate merger in history
January 10

First all-electrified service begins between Boston and Washington, D.C., with Train 131 completing the trip without changing power
January 31

Online passenger ticket sales grow to $63 million, 5.1 percent of total automated ticket sales

Northeast High Speed Rail Improvement Project to electrify the North End is completed

Ridership on newly electrified regional service to Boston grows by 45 percent, and revenues jump 77 percent

HotLinks names Amtrak.com "one of the most bookmarked sites on the web"

2001

When launched, *Acela* advertising was edgy and designed to create a new image for Amtrak and its new service.

2001

First *Acela Express*
trainset enters service
December 11

November 7
George W. Bush elected 43rd
president of the United States

January 15
Wikipedia launches

Amtrak photo

Compared at the time to a blockbuster movie premiere, the start of *Acela Express* service in December 2000 began with great fanfare.

In its first year of operation, *Acela Express* service carries 2,473,921 riders, almost 500,000 more than predicted

Just before the Thanksgiving rush, "Julie," automated voice response technology, is launched on 1-800-USA-RAIL

September 11
Al-Qaeda suicide attacks take place in United States, destroying the World Trade Center and killing almost 3,000 people

Three generations of power are shown in three liveries: from left, a new power car of an *Acela Express* electric trainset, a 1990s P40 in Amtrak's fourth locomotive paint scheme (Phase IV), and a 1980s F40 with a Phase III paint scheme await their next assignment at Boston's Southampton Street Maintenance Facility.

Amtrak trains serve a variety of stations, some with boarding platforms the same height as railcar doors and others that require a step box. Here, Conductor Greg Moss lends a hand in Alexandria, Va.

Ticket Agent Joe Munn greets passengers with a smile while on duty at Washington Union Station.

Company announces that it is 6 weeks away from insolvency

Amtrak reorganizes and eliminates Strategic Business Units and duplicative functions

U.S. Department of Transportation loan agreement to rescue Amtrak from bankruptcy is signed

December 15
Amtrak's *Downeaster Service* is inaugurated between Portland, Maine, and Boston

Acela trainsets and HHP-8 locomotives are removed from service due to yaw damper bracket malfunctions

Silver Palm is renamed *Palmetto*

Amtrak photo

U.S. Department of Homeland Security
becomes a new Cabinet-level department
November 25

Columbia space shuttle disaster occurs
February 1

October 2
U.S. Congress authorizes the
president to use force in Iraq

2002 closes with
another ridership record

Matt Donnelly

Gregory Weirich

Through the decade, Amtrak partnerships with state agencies grew to 15 states, including service increases on the three routes shown here. The *San Diegans* (above) between Los Angeles and San Diego became the *Pacific Surfliner* in 2000, using distinctive ocean-blue, state-owned railcars and becoming one of the nation's busiest corridors. Using railcars and locomotives mostly owned by state partners in Washington and Oregon, *Cascades* (right) provides transportation despite snow and ice in the Pacific Northwest. The *Downeaster* (left) serves Portland, Maine, in a restoration of service that has served as an example to many states that lost their intercity passenger trains prior to Amtrak.

Charlie Monte Verde: The Loyal Steward

A lot of people talk about having loved trains as kids. They talk about the elaborate model train layouts they constructed in their basements. They enumerate train fan newsletters and magazines they pored over every month. They enthuse about their cross-country sleeping car trips, starting in Washington, D.C., on the *Capitol Limited*, changing in Chicago to the *Texas Eagle*, and then switching to the *Sunset Limited* to disembark in Los Angeles. And then there is Charlie Monte Verde.

You can see him here—not yet school age—young Charlie Monte Verde beginning his railroad education at his train station hometown in Rochester, N.Y.

Although he looks every bit the well-groomed, perfectly ordinary boy next door, Charlie is anything but ordinary when it comes to trains. He comes from a family of railfans, was raised as a railfan, constructed his formal education around the study of trains, built his career and personal life around trains, and—it seems safe to say—that as long as there are trains at all, Charlie will remain their loyal steward. That could be a long haul: he isn't even 30 yet.

"When people ask me how long I've been involved in the railroad business, I tell them about my dad changing my diapers in the rail yard," he chuckles. Charlie's father, David Monte Verde, is the president of his own railroad, Genesee Valley Transportation (GVT Rail), which runs short line railroads in New York and Pennsylvania. Railroading, it seems, is in their blood.

Growing up near Rochester, David's boyhood years were set to the rhythms of the *Phoebe Snow* of the Lackawanna Railroad, the train that wound through the Genesee Valley and made a stop at his childhood home of Dansville, N.Y. When it stopped running, along with all the other passenger trains in his area, David, 16 at the time, made up his mind to save them. By the late 1980s, his company was awarded a contract to operate a five-mile spur of that same Lackawanna Railroad in Erie County, N.Y., and David went along steadily adding to his railroad properties for the next two decades. Today, GVT Rail owns or operates more than 300 miles of rail lines in upstate New York and northeastern Pennsylvania, operating a fleet of 30 locomotives and eight terminals.
Running a small, privately owned

railroad was tough in the early years when Charlie was small. "When my dad first started, it was a four person company," he recalls. "If a customer needed switching at 3 a.m., you were the one who had to go out and do it." When Charlie, the eldest of three boys, was young, his father was the one doing such jobs—along with all the negotiations and administration. As a kid, Charlie admits that he was "always chasing trains, taking pictures of them, videotaping them"—sticking as closely to his Dad as time and safety permitted. "I wanted to taste it all—to experience all of it," he says, with infectious zeal.

At 13, Charlie was accompanying his father to railroad board meetings in Scranton, Pa., and he began to develop a sense of the industry's inner machinations. When he graduated from high school, Charlie joined track workers to paint all the warning signals on the line. "To this day, every once in awhile, I'll still see some of that silver paint on my clothes," he laughs.

As the boss's son, he knew that he could ask for a desk job at the company, skip the years of manual toil that his father had endured, and skate his way to the top. But he didn't want to go that route. "If you're going to be the president of a small railroad company, and you're interacting with track laborers, you have

to know what they do," he stresses. "I wanted to understand how hard the job really was, how it all worked."

For the next several summers, Charlie built and maintained track. In the fall and winter, he swept snow out of switch points. In the spring, he cleared brush. "By being in the track department, maybe you make less and break your back more, but at the end of the day, you built something," he marvels. "You realize that the new track, rails, and ties you were laying would be there for 50 or 60 years." He loved it.

In fact, David became concerned that Charlie loved track work too much. He urged his son to complete his college degree, and Charlie reluctantly agreed—until he realized that he could study transportation. At Empire State College in New York, Charlie researched policy and urban transit systems, focusing mainly on the dynamics of light rail systems and subsidized public transportation. After Charlie graduated in 2008, his undergraduate work and life experience on the railroad allowed him to secure an internship, and then a job as a legislative assistant specializing in transportation issues, for New York State Senator James S. Alesi.

But the heavy rails were still tied tightly around Charlie's heart. So, when an opportunity to work for Amtrak as a government affairs specialist opened up, Charlie didn't even have to think about it: It was, he says, as if all his passions, field experience, and academic research were magically combined into a single job description. Working out of Amtrak's Chicago Government Affairs office, Charlie and his colleagues build and support state and local relationships, getting to know elected officials and community leaders from the Appalachians to the Rockies, and from Oklahoma to the Canadian border. In the mere nine months that he's worked at Amtrak, he says, he has traveled by train to 18 states on company business.

What's more, he is somehow learning even more about the railroad industry. "I'm extremely lucky to be in this position," he says. "I've learned more in nine months at Amtrak than I have at any other point in my life." For a guy who has been working on the railroad since he was in diapers, that's saying something.

March 19
Military invasion of Iraq begins

In California, Amtrak and Caltrans contract with private operators to offer connecting motorcoach service in an extensive network that reaches where the trains cannot go, such as Fisherman's Wharf in San Francisco.

Doug Riddell

Amtrak photo

Passengers count on train attendants such as Karen Miller to greet them with a smile and be of assistance, whether their stop is at noon or at midnight.

Amtrak photo

Using recipes developed in the Amtrak test kitchens in Wilmington, Del., Regional Chef Hashim Abdul-Salaam rides the rails to provide instruction and assistance to onboard service crews.

Steve Ostrowski

In Jacksonville, Fla., during a special trip to explore service expansion in Florida, Danell Huthsing helps stock Amtrak car 10031, the railroad's only remaining Great Dome.

Amtrak closes
the year with
record ridership

Facebook is
founded
February 4

Head count drops
below 20,000 for the
first time in 2 decades

Average U.S. price of
a gallon of unleaded
gas reaches $2

December 18
Downtown Richmond
station opens for expanded
Tidewater service

Acela Express Quiet Car
service is introduced
on weekends

Acela Express adds new
frequencies, and new *Blue
Water* service is launched

Amtrak and Pennsylvania announce pla[?]
to improve and rehabilitate the Keyston[?]
Corridor, increasing speeds to 110 mph

TRAIN INFORMATION

6:34 time

Time	Number	Train	To	From	Status	Track
6:35	1646	SHORE LINE EAST	NEW LONDON	NEW HAVEN	ALL ABOARD	10
6:38	2173	ACELA EXPRESS	WASHINGTON	BOSTON	10 mins LATE	
6:57	1587	METRO-NORTH	GRAND CENTRAL	NEW HAVEN	ON TIME	14
7:00	1656	SHORE LINE EAST	OLD SAYBROOK	NEW HAVEN	ON TIME	10
7:20	94	REGIONAL	BOSTON	NEWPORT NEWS	ON TIME	
7:23	2193	ACELA EXPRESS	NEW YORK	BOSTON	ON TIME	
7:25	494	REGIONAL	SPRINGFIELD	NEW HAVEN	ON TIME	

· PASSENGERS PLEASE WATCH YOUR BELONGINGS / SECURITY
· WILL REMOVE ANY UNATTENDED BAGS

solari s.c. udine, italy
systems america

Doug Riddell

The distinct "flap-flap-flap" sound of the ever-changing Solari arrival and departure board can still be heard at the New Haven, Conn., station, where *Acela Express, Northeast Regional,* and other trains converge.

Doug Riddell

A passenger purchases a ticket as the late afternoon sun shines in the historic New Haven station.

Acela Express schedules improve, and all weekend Northeast Corridor trains become reserved

Palmetto service south of Savannah is discontinued as mail contract ends
November 1

Station opens at Milwaukee's General Mitchell International Airport

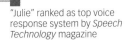
"Julie" ranked as top voice response system by *Speech Technology* magazine

February 10
North Korea announces it has nuclear weapons

Matt Donnelly

To support the operation of thousands of Amtrak and commuter trains that use the high-voltage catenary system on the Northeast and Keystone corridors day-in and day-out, inspection and maintenance work takes place in the off-hours using a specialized maintenance vehicle nicknamed the "cat car."

Gary Pancavage

Maintenance takes place under the trains as well. Here, Pipefitter David Place works under an *Acela Express* trainset in Sunnyside Yard, Queens, N.Y.

Harris Cohen

As the use of digital music players, mobile phones, and laptop computers grew through the 2000s, many passengers applauded the creation of Quiet Cars on several trains, including the *Acela Express*.

Advertising is often seen as disposable instead of collectable, but the mid-decade decision by Amtrak to commission graphic artist Michael Schwab resulted in works so sought after that they were sold on Amtrak.com. This collection features an *Acela Express* poster, a series of posters for overnight trains, a travel poster for *San Joaquins*, and the first National Train Day poster from 2008.

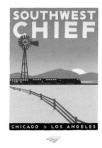

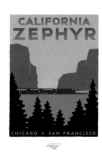

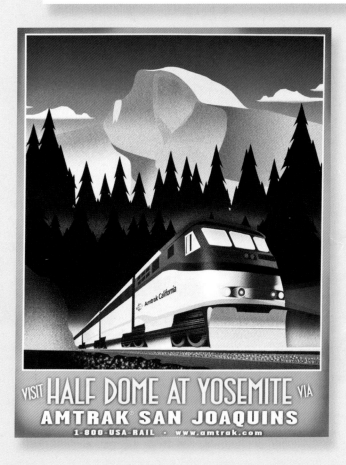

Administration proposes to "zero out" Amtrak for FY 2006 budget

In the wake of Hurricane Katrina, *Sunset Limited* service east of New Orleans is suspended indefinitely

China completes railway to Tibet, setting a record for highest railroad in the world
October 15

Northeast Regional trains become all-reserved

New auto carriers for the *Auto Train* enter service

Acela Express trainsets go out of service due to cracks found in brake rotors

FY 2005 ridership sets record for third consecutive year

Amtrak photo

As part of a joint program to raise speeds and upgrade service on the Keystone Line between Philadelphia and Harrisburg, Amtrak workers replaced and realigned tracks for higher speeds. The Switch Exchange System gang is seen realigning the station tracks at Lancaster to allow trains to approach and depart this historic station at faster speeds.

Matt Donnelly

Winter doesn't stop trains, but it can stop switches from working. To keep switches free from snow and ice in terminals, the hot exhaust from snow jets is used to keep things moving freely.

Phil Gosney

Amtrak, the Capital Corridor Joint Powers Authority, and Union Pacific (UP) formed a partnership to increase capacity and reliability on the UP in the Northern California Bay area. The result was an increase in the number of trains.

John Eschenbach collection

Over Amtrak's 40 year history, many improvements were made not only to the NEC but to a number of other heavy passenger lines around the country as well. John Eschenbach, a 34-year Amtrak veteran is seen checking the track gauge of a recently completed project in southern California.

California, Washington, Illinois, and Pennsylvania launch new state-supported Amtrak services

Agreement is signed with Long Island Rail Road and Metropolitan Transit Authority to support East Side Access project

Capitol Corridor adds 4 new round trips between Sacramento and Oakland and 3 between Oakland and San Jose

Three Rivers service west of Pittsburgh is discontinued

Spanish-language Amtrak.com website launches

Estimated $60 million is saved through Strategic Reform Initiatives during the year

June 3
Montenegro declares independence from Serbia

Jason Berg

Amtrak puts more mileage on its cars and locomotives than any other railroad in the United States. With up to 25,000 miles per month on each P42, a lot of road grime and dirt accumulates. Here, unit 164 takes a bath in the Seattle car wash.

Mike Latiff: In Moments of Crisis, Memories of a Career

It was just another morning in Miami for Mike Latiff. More than a decade into his Amtrak career, he'd moved from Washington, D.C., to manage the company's *Silver Service*, in charge of crews that ran up the East Coast to New York City and back down again.

His cell phone rang. "Turn on your television," said a friend, who then described a dramatic lower Manhattan scene: the airplane that struck the World Trade Center, the tower that had already collapsed, and the thick purple plume of smoke.

"What movie is that?" Mike asked.

This was real. In Amtrak's Miami office, and in offices across the United States, a realization of what would later be known simply as 9/11 began to form.

"Initially, nobody could grasp how big this was," Mike recalls. "But I knew right away that, being a government entity and a provider of mass transit, we—all of us at Amtrak—would most likely be called into service. We needed to mobilize." He and his family were safe. So Mike's mind focused in one direction: "Where is my crew? How can I get them back to Miami?"

Air travel was grounded with no word on when airports would reopen. Rail service was shut down, too, for a few hours. But following necessary inspections of bridges, tracks, and signals, the trains began rolling again. "It really became clear that Amtrak was going to be the only transportation choice in and out of New York City," Mike says. "Not much else was moving."

Rolling stock was scraped up and hastily rerouted from distant corners of the Amtrak system to the Northeast. Mike helped pull two or three trains together, forming a "supertrain" of sorts. He tracked down his crew and prepared them for a long and arduous trip.

Cell phones weren't much good, the lines were mostly jammed. A television in the conference room offered a steady stream of updates. A national conference call connected various operations centers, the corporate office in Washington, and the Amtrak Police Department.

The day unfolded with an odd rhythm— tense conversations, quick decisions, and lots of waiting. In those extended pauses— for a call from a crew member, for another piece to fall into place along his route—Mike reflected on the unlikely course that had led him to this moment.

He'd never intended to get into the train business. When he'd arrived in Washington,

D.C., in 1989, from Trinidad, via a brief stint working in hotels, he had yet to set foot on a passenger train. A job at Amtrak sounded interesting for a short stint, he figured, after which he would move on.

Yet that first employee ride from Washington, D.C., to Cumberland, Md., turned his head around. When the train reached Harpers Ferry, W.Va., the sight of the Potomac and Shenandoah Rivers below, and the feeling of rolling along above, nearly took his breath away. "This might not be so bad," he remembers thinking. Even today, whenever Mike rides that line, if he can find a seat, he doesn't get up until after Harpers Ferry. That view and that sensation never get old.

Right off, Mike enjoyed working as a member of the *Capitol Limited*'s onboard service staff. Back in 1989, the line was still composed largely of aging Heritage cars, which made the trip—overnight from D.C. to Chicago and then back to D.C.—a challenging one.

"Once you got on board, there was always some adventure," he says. Just a few months into his career, already a chef in the dining car, Mike worked a train that got stuck in the snow for five hours near Canton, Ohio. The power was out. While the crew awaited a rescue engine, they kept passengers as warm and well fed as possible. "It was an experience in what I've come to love most about this company," Mike says. "Teamwork."

Before long, Amtrak began presenting Mike with unanticipated opportunities. A special course at the Culinary Institute of America, studying with stellar chefs, taught him specific skills, the correct way to julienne a carrot, for instance, as well as deeper lessons. "I didn't just take what I absorbed to work," he says. "I took it home. I took it through my life."

Two years later, he was a ticket clerk at Washington Union Station and then lead ticket agent, the beginning of a long association with Amtrak station management. In 1999, then Director of Station Planning Ellen Taylor, who was preparing the Northeast Corridor stations for the arrival of the high-speed *Acela Service* line, asked Mike to join her group. The *Acela Service* represented an ambitious gamble: that Amtrak could develop efficient high-speed service, that the American people would take to it, and that the line would improve the company's financial position at a sagging moment in the train business.

"There was excitement," Mike recalls, "but there were also naysayers." As project coordinator, he had to ensure that when the sleek trains bearing the silver-and-teal *Acela* logo rolled into one of the eight stations on which he worked, passengers would recognize the brand as something exciting, combining the cachet of great trains past with the promise of the future. More than a year of planning— attention to every last detail, from new signage to special lighting—went into the moment when fireworks lit the sky outside Washington Union Station and the *Acela Express* set off. "It was a huge production," Mike says. "If passenger trains had been a dying industry, this was going to be its renaissance."

Mike's eyes still widen when recalling that excitement, a decade later, after more than 20 years at Amtrak. But nothing makes them alight as much as the memory of that day in September when the country called, and Amtrak answered.

This chapter of Amtrak history had few naysayers. "After the FAA grounded all flights following the terrorist attacks, travelers turned to Amtrak," Indiana Representative Julia May Carson reported to Congress on June 11, 2002. "Whether people had to travel for business, to help with rescue efforts, or just to get home, Amtrak kept our American citizens moving during a time of national emergency."

Mike, now a senior officer in the Policy and Development department's Station Design and Planning group, remembers what that effort felt like, minute by minute. "My adrenaline was running so high, I wasn't even scared," he says. "I just kept thinking about how to get these people moving. The second week of September would typically be a quiet one for the trains in my region. Students were already in school, and parents were back home. Instead, we had our busiest day. And our finest hour."

Mechanical department overhauls
178 passenger cars, 45 locomotives,
and 17 electric locomotives

North Korea claims a
successful nuclear test
October 9

Intergovernmental Panel on Climate
Change publishes a report attributing
climate change to human causes
February 2

Amtrak police focus on community
policing, with increased presence at
gates, on platforms, and aboard trains

With a record Thanksgiving, the highest
revenue month to date is recorded

Amtrak President Joe Boardman says hello to Conductor Sam Bens, who is working on a train between Virginia and Washington, D.C.

Veteran Amtrak Police Chief John O'Connor and other Amtrak police officers inspect security at Washington Union Station.

As baby boomers begin to retire in the 2000s, Amtrak has been facing a large need to replace experienced railroaders. Conductor trainee Margaret Gobel learns how to properly throw a hand-operated switch in the yard at Los Angeles.

101

In Illinois, 8 new trains are inaugurated and 28 downstate stops added

Great American Stations website launches to foster partnerships with local communities wishing to invest in their stations

Amtrak wins "2007 Image of the Year Award" by the National Association of Uniform Manufacturers and Distributors

Diner Lites and diner-lounges (Cross Country Café) are response to mandated food and beverage cost reduction

Electrified service begins on Keystone Service; trips increase from 11 to 14 and speeds reach 110 mph

Quik-Trak machine wins "Best Travel and Hospitality Deployment" from Kioskcom's Self Service Excellence Awards

Average price of a gallon of unleaded reaches $3 for the first time

At-seat cart and beverage service starts on some *Acela Express* trains

Gary Pancavage

To renew Amtrak's fleet, 10 new GP15D locomotives were purchased in 2004 for work train and yard service. These new fuel-efficient locomotives helped Amtrak retire some of its oldest locomotives, some that dated back to 1940.

Doug Riddell

A passenger at Washington Union Station uses the latest Quik-Trak self-service ticket machine, launched in 2007. These award-winning, ADA-compliant kiosks make ticketing or purchasing a reservation even more convenient.

Doug Riddell

As ridership climbed to record levels, new auto carriers were introduced in 2005, and a new *Auto Train* terminal in Sanford, Fla., opened in 2010.

Amtrak.com accounts for 42 percent of ticket sales; Quick-Trak accounts for 7 percent of ticket sales and 32 percent of tickets issued

Settlements are reached with unions following recommendations of the Presidential Emergency Board in fall

Average price of a gallon of unleaded reaches $4 for the first time

Deployment of Mobile Security Teams initiated to patrol trains and conduct random screening of passengers and carry-on baggage

A record Thanksgiving becomes the largest to date

14 states contract with Amtrak for service delivery, representing nearly half of daily departures

May 10
Amtrak holds its first National Train Day

Jason Berg

P42 locomotive 160 was placed into service on May 1, 2001, Amtrak's 30th anniversary. It is one of Amtrak's 207 third-generation P42 diesel locomotives, which carried the railroad through its 40th anniversary.

These representative ad campaigns from the 2000s highlight the convenience and benefits of Amtrak versus other modes of transportation.

Thames River Bridge
lift span replacement
is completed

Washington Union
Station celebrates its
centennial anniversary

Congress passes
Passenger Rail Investment
and Improvement Act

President-elect Barack Obama and vice-
president-elect Joe Biden travel on Amtrak
to Washington, D.C., for their inauguration
January 17

Wind power generator and solar
panels are installed in Chicago
yard to power signal system

Milwaukee Intermodal Station
is renovated, and St. Louis
Gateway Station opens

November 11
Oceanliner Queen
Elizabeth 2 completes her
last commercial voyage

In 2008, Amtrak completed one of its largest ever single capital projects. The 90-year-old Thames River Bridge in New London, Conn., was converted from a bascule span to a lift span during a four-day period.

Roger Riley, Amtrak Engineering

Washington Union Station opened in 1908 and was shared by the many railroads. In 2008, Amtrak celebrated the 100th anniversary of the station with five historic locomotives posed at the Ivy City Maintenance Facility.

Shawn Gordon

American Recovery and
Reinvestment Act provides $1.3 billion
for investment in Amtrak system

H1N1 virus is classified as a global pandemic
by the World Health Organization

June 11

New or renovated stations
open at Durham, Picayune,
Saco, and Leavenworth

Commonwealth of Virginia funds extension of
daily *Northeast Regional Service* to Lynchburg,
bringing total of state-supported services to 15

Nearly 50 percent of daily
services are state-supported

June 25
Pop singer Michael Jackson dies

Doug Riddell

Amtrak Spokesperson Tracy Connell
talks to the media at 30th Street Station
in Philadelphia during a high-speed rail
conference.

Manuel Vega

On January 17, 2009, President-elect Obama greets crew members Barbara
Hague, Kelly Pitts, Martina Brewbaker, and Teresa Hughey at his inaugural train
in Philadelphia, Pa., before it departs for Washington, D.C.

Courtney Ware

Virginia became the 15th state to support Amtrak services. The new round trip to Lynchburg was an extension of
existing Northeast Corridor service that proved to be so popular that Virginia would not have to pay any subsidies
for the operation of the train.

Amtrak commits to installing Positive Train Control technology on the Northeast Corridor and the Michigan Line by 2012

71 percent farebox recovery is the highest reported among passenger and commuter railroads in the U.S.

An earthquake measuring 7.0 on the Richter scale devastates Haiti
January 12

Safe-2-Safer initiative launched to improve security and reduce injuries

Amtrak launches Mobility First program to make stations more accessible

Administration announces award of $7.92 billion for high-speed and intercity passenger rail services in 31 states

April 20
Deepwater Horizon oil platform explodes and burns in the Gulf of Mexico, leading to a 3-month oil s

2000s

Fiscal Year	Ridership	Stations Served	Passenger Miles (Millions)	Revenue (Millions)
2000	22,517,264	515	5,897	1,088
2001	23,493,805	512	6,160	1,178
2002	23,406,597	515	5,654	1,250
2003	24,028,119	514	5,358	1,183
2004	25,053,564	517	5,391	1,231
2005	25,374,998	518	5,558	1,216
2006	24,392,065	503	5,503	1,371
2007	25,847,531	497	5,468	1,519
2008	28,716,407	527	5,559	1,734
2009	27,167,014	527	5,498	1,599
2010	28,716,857	528	6,332	1,743

Collin King

Amtrak Police Officer Edward Ross is seen with his K-9 partner Zeta outside Washington Union Station. Zeta is one of 46 K-9 employees protecting a nation in transit.

Doug Riddell

Through the late 2000s, Amtrak continued to break ridership records. The second busiest station on the Amtrak system is Washington, D.C., seen here with passengers waiting for a northbound train.

William Shaffer

In 2010, Amtrak, the Federal Railway Administration, and Oklahoma DOT began a pilot program to use biofuel in passenger locomotives. Test locomotive 500 is seen pushing the *Heartland Flyer* out of Fort Worth on its way to Oklahoma City.

Metrolink commuter service
resumes operation

Contract is announced for purchasing
130 new sleeping, dining, baggage,
and baggage-dormitory cars

Acela Express marks
its 10th anniversary

Free Wi-Fi service debuts at New York Penn
Station, Washington Union Station, and other
stations as well as on all *Acela Express* trains

Running on 20 percent biodiesel fuel, the
Heartland Flyer becomes one of *Time*
magazine's 50 Best Inventions of 2010

Amtrak unveils NextGen
High Speed Rail Study

Matt Donnelly

A northbound *Acela Express* train pauses at the station in Wilmington, Del., in the evening on its way from Washington, D.C., to Boston.

Matt Donnelly

To celebrate its 40th
anniversary, Amtrak
painted each of its
previous paint schemes
on P42 locomotives.
No. 145 is seen on the
point of the *Silver Meteor*
at Jacksonville, Fla., wearing the Phase III scheme.

An early morning *Acela Express* train swiftly rolls across the Susquehanna River Bridge.

the fu

Gary Pancavage

The Way Forward

I HOPE THIS BOOK has introduced you to the rich panorama of Amtrak—taken from every angle of the camera lens and from many corners of our far-reaching operation. Each decade adds a rich layer of experience, and each story comes from another perspective. I hope you've enjoyed looking at the last 40 years of our company's history; it's a rich one, filled with all the excitement, surprises, and transitions of a long journey by rail.

It's also filled with our people. The variety of voices is a product of the rich diversity of a company that serves places as distant from one another as Seattle, San Diego, Miami, and Portland, Maine— practically the four corners

Joe Boardman

of America. They speak in the accents of every region, and of all the varieties and types of work that are necessary to keep Amtrak running—because that's a vital task, one that I'm proud to say many people have devoted their lives to.

I am Amtrak's ninth president and CEO; I took the job in November 2008. In that short time, I have come to deeply appreciate what this company means—to American transportation, to the communities we serve, and to the more than 28 million passengers who rode our trains during FY 2010. This book is a tribute to the people who built the national intercity passenger rail system and to all of those who help keep it running: the workers, policymakers, citizens, passengers, and the people who are even now working to sustain and develop our system. They will build upon the work that has been done, for that's what healthy companies do: they celebrate significant milestones and turn them into the foundation for future successes. Not many companies survive for 40 years—and those that do survive because they have talented people, a great product, and a strong history marked by initiative, endurance, competence, and success.

Amtrak can claim a very rich history indeed: some of our services trace their roots to the very beginnings of the railroad in America. There are still a few—a very few—people here who began their railroad careers in the last days of steam, and there are plenty of employees who can remember each of the great transitions that have marked Amtrak's history: the company's formation, the transfer of the Northeast Corridor in 1976, and the beginning of the *Acela Express* service. This is why we insist so ardently that our employees are the true strength of our product.

Our employees have been more than the witnesses to what was in fact a revolutionary transformation—they were the people who brought it about, and when we say that the company has changed greatly since May 1, 1971, that statement is a tribute to them. People supplied the dynamism and the energy that kept the company from stagnating, and they took the initiative to develop the creative vision that gave us successful products like *Acela Express*. And they did it on a stringent budget, one that demanded they find creative ways to alter and improve bridges, track, and electrical systems that were designed with something altogether different in mind. Today, we must address ourselves to the task of ensuring that the changes we make in the coming years will help us meet the needs of our customers and ensure our company stays vigorous, competent, and competitive well into the future.

The first and the greatest change will come very soon, and that will be the generational transition. Of all the challenges we face, it is the most certain because it is driven by the unavoidable limits of our working lives. New people are already coming into our business, and we must be sure that the lessons they learn as they arrive are the right ones—for those experiences will be formative and enduring.

We must also make sure that the working environment welcomes the young, who have grown up in a world that's very different from the world people of my age knew. Customers will continue to demand ever-better service; employees want a modern workplace. These are justified demands, and we must keep pace with that evolution if we are to offer our employees the environment they deserve and our customers the journeys they expect. Customer expectation must drive our planning because our business exists to satisfy a demand—not only the customer's demand for better and more comfortable transportation, but the nation's need for mobility alternatives that will keep America competitive and healthy. Amtrak and intercity passenger rail can offer consumers an appealing alternative to a clogged highway system or an air travel model that's composed in equal parts of delay, discomfort, and disrobing. Since 2002, we have carried more people between New York and Washington than all of the airlines put together. Since 2009, we can say the same about our New York to Boston service. These are examples of what Amtrak can do, and we're working with state partners to replicate these successes wherever we can find a market and partners with vision and the courage to try new alternatives.

Our Northeast Corridor is a tremendous success—but we still live in an environment in which our budgets are never certain, and their levels are hard to predict, and we're confined by engineering decisions that were made a century ago. To address this need, we have prepared a vision for a "Next Generation High Speed Rail" plan for the Northeast—something with the potential to free our services from the speed and capacity constraints of an aging infrastructure and transform the largest regional passenger system in America into a high-speed railroad that will be the equal of anything in the world.

The system we envision will follow the same route as the existing railroad—but it will enter cities like Philadelphia and Baltimore on a new line that will bring improved levels of service to city centers. North of New York, the new route will sweep away from the existing route, avoiding the curves of our current line up the Connecticut coast, and cross the center of New England on an alignment that will permit 220 mph speeds. This is a grand vision, and it won't be inexpensive. What it will be is successful. I'm confident that such a system will draw an enormous number of riders because I've seen what we can do on the NEC with minimal resources and under very challenging conditions. The demand is there; if we can supply an even better product, people will use it.

These are not small plans; a 220 mph railroad in the Northeast would be the greatest rail construction project in a century. We know we can do it. As you look through the pages of this book, you can get a sense for the challenges the men and women of Amtrak have faced—and surmounted—over the last 40 years. They met the challenge of conceiving, planning, and inaugurating the Amtrak system. They saw the possibilities inherent in the Northeast Corridor when it was not much more than a ragged and rusty castoff from Penn Central. They set to work to improve it and to turn our Washington to New York line into a 125 mph railroad. When that was done, they took on the even bigger task of electrifying the Boston to New Haven line—and succeeded in making the high-speed electric railroad that our predecessors envisioned a century before.

They rebuilt the fleet to eliminate the last vestiges of the steam age and then built a new fleet to replace it; today, they are working at the giant task of replacing our equipment yet again. We're starting with the single-level, long-distance cars to ensure that customers continue to enjoy the service and accommodations that have given us a whole series of annual ridership records. We're also replacing our electric locomotive fleet to maintain the hard-won record for reliability our people have built through the *Northeast Regional Service*.

New equipment will mean better products for our customers, and easier lives for our employees, whose tasks will be eased considerably when we can finally retire the aging and hard-run cars of the Heritage Fleet after 60 years of service.

These accomplishments matter—and they're not simply products of the larger economy or of congestion on other modes. They are something that the men and women of Amtrak brought about through hard work, patience, and above all, through commitment to the challenge of building, running, and developing our railroad and providing our country with the transportation choices it will need in the future.

We love the railroad—but we're not just doing these things because we enjoy them. We're doing them because America needs Amtrak. Our country needs safer, greener, and healthier transportation alternatives, and passenger rail can provide them. Amtrak doesn't just promise it—we deliver it, and our record of fuel-efficiency, safety, and comfort explains why Americans are flocking to Amtrak in record numbers. We often think of trains as the mode of travel people preferred in days gone by, and this book has told you why. But we hope it will also explain something that's just as important: that in these days of traffic jams and air rage, there is a better travel alternative out there, one that preserves the pleasures that once made people want to travel while addressing our very modern concerns about the environment, our time, and our pocketbooks. That alternative is Amtrak—and I hope that after reading this book, you'll have a sense not only of what we have always offered America but what we will provide in the years to come.

Joe Boardman is president and chief executive officer of Amtrak, a position he has held since 2008. Prior to coming to Amtrak, he was administrator of the Federal Railroad Administration and commissioner of the New York State Department of Transportation.

A Day in the Life of Amtrak

PASSENGERS WHO RIDE AMTRAK probably don't spend a lot of time thinking about who makes their train run and how. For many riders, Amtrak employees consist of the friendly conductor who punches their ticket, the attendant who serves a hot cup of coffee in the café car, and the baggage handler who helps with their luggage at the destination. And that's how it should be. At its best, rail travel should be as effortless as being driven in a luxury automobile. To the riding public, Amtrak employees should always remain a steady, helpful, informative but unobtrusive part of the journey.

Behind the scenes, Amtrak employees see themselves in a different light. Coast to coast, over 20,000 Amtrak employees work around the clock every day of the year ensuring that the trains America depends on run safely and on time. At any hour of the day, someone somewhere in the Amtrak system is hard at work—carrying out his or her job to the very best of one's ability. The tasks are varied—a welder creates metal shielding for the undercarriage of a car, a chef tries out a new sandwich that will remain fresh and appealing while the dining car that carries it moves through two time zones and back, a manager provides a safety briefing to a crew of experienced men and women for what may likely be an exhausting overnight run. Because of their nature, some of these jobs garner acknowledgment. Some of the jobs are unsung. But from the offices at Amtrak's Washington, D.C., headquarters to the ticket counters in Chicago Union Station and to the maintenance facility in Oakland, Calif., each Amtrak employee understands that he or she plays a role in the vast and complicated daily choreography required to maintain America's passenger trains.

This section of the book is an attempt to open a window onto this world: Amtrak workers in action. During a few days in October 2010, employees were asked to take photographs of Amtrak operations and send them in. The response was staggering. More than 100 employees from 30 states submitted images. There were snapshots of colleagues gathered by the vending machine, working at desks, making up beds in sleeping cars, monitoring trains on multicolor screens, and in uniform and on patrol. There were classic compositions of hard-hat-wearing track workers dwarfed by greasy machines. And action shots of conductors helping passengers board and, later, exit the train. The quality of the photographs was varied, but if the light meter failed, the enthusiasm for the company where the photographers worked was undiminished. And slowly, as we sifted through the photographs, a strong hour-by-hour portrait of a vital, thriving, energetic, and determined workforce began to emerge.

Limited space and time meant that not all of the wonderful photographs that were submitted made it into the book. But no one's contribution was overlooked or forgotten. With permission, each image will become part of the permanent archive of the railroad. These photographs tell a story of hard work, endurance, and dedication. We think it's a story that our employees, our passengers, and our country deserves to hear.

12:20 A.M. START OF THE JOURNEY. Two passengers wait for the *City of New Orleans* in Newbern, Tenn. Newbern is one of the smaller communities that rely on Amtrak as its principal intercity travel option. This destination is known as a flag stop—trains stop here only on an as-needed or requested basis if there are passengers to pick up or drop off; otherwise, the train bypasses the station.

12:26 A.M. WAITING FOR A TRAIN. In Walnut Ridge, Ark., a passenger and a friend wait for the southbound *Texas Eagle*. Shortly before dawn, the train will reunite this passenger with a long-lost family member.

12:21 A.M. LOADING IT UP. Station Agent Maryann Dianni in Rochester, N.Y., wears rubberized work gloves to make it easier for loading and unloading baggage on and off the westbound *Lake Shore Limited.*

12:30 A.M. **SEAT OF POWER. From her office near Penn Station, Dispatcher Eva Gonzalez controls train traffic moving to and from New York City. Her job requires nerves of steel and constant vigilance to ensure safe passage on one of the nation's busiest stretches of track.**

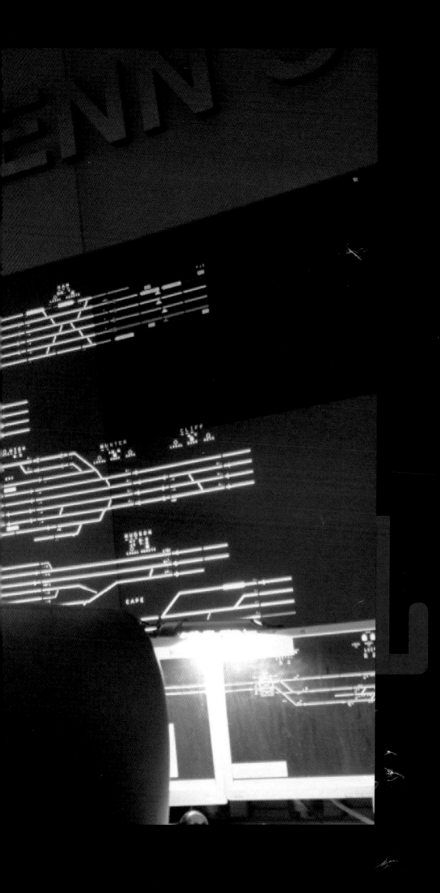

Amtrak facts

Amtrak operates a nationwide rail network, serving more than 500 destinations in 46 states and three Canadian provinces on more than 21,200 miles of routes, with more than 20,000 employees. It is the nation's only high-speed intercity passenger rail provider, operating nearly 60 percent of its trains at speeds in excess of 90 mph.

In fiscal year 2010 (October 2009 to September 2010), Amtrak welcomed aboard more than 28.7 million passengers, the largest annual total in Amtrak's history. An average of 78,000 passengers rode 300 Amtrak trains per day.

In FY 2010, Amtrak earned approximately $2.51 billion in revenue and incurred approximately $3.74 billion in expenses. No country in the world operates a passenger rail system without some form of public support for capital costs and/or operating expenses. In 2009 (the most recent year for which data of other railroads is available), Amtrak's farebox recovery (percentage of operating costs covered by revenues generated by passenger fares) was the highest reported for any U.S. passenger railroad.

In 2009, an average of more than 925,000 people every weekday rode commuter trains operated by Amtrak under contracts with local or regional agencies or depended on commuter rail services that used Amtrak-owned infrastructure, Amtrak dispatching, or shared operations.

Amtrak's Northeast Corridor (NEC) is the busiest railroad in North America with more than 2,200 trains operating over some portion of the Washington-Boston route each day. More than 250,000 riders use the NEC every weekday, generating more than 4.9 million daily passenger miles.

If included among U.S. airlines in 2008, Amtrak would rank eighth in the number of passengers served. On average, there are nearly twice as many passengers on an Amtrak train than there are on a domestic airline flight.

The Boston-New York-Washington portion of the Northeast Corridor carried 10,375,209 passengers in FY 2010 on *Acela Express*, *Regional Service*, or other trains. Three other corridors had ridership topping one million: *Pacific Surfliner Service* (San Diego-Los Angeles-San Luis Obispo: 2,613,604), *Capitol Corridor Service* (San Jose-Oakland-Sacramento-Auburn: 1,580,619), and *Keystone Corridor Service* (Harrisburg-Philadelphia-New York City: 1,296,838).

1:00 A.M. NIGHT SERVICE. The northbound *Auto Train*, which goes from central Florida to suburban Washington, D.C., makes its one and only stop in Florence, S.C. While passengers sleep, the train attendants fill the train with fresh water and fuel and welcome a new train crew.

An average of

78,000

passengers ride

300

1:05 A.M. SAFETY FIRST. From her vantage point in the inspection pit in Boston's Southampton Street Yard, Mechanic Margaret O'Neil-Simone examines the underside of an *Acela Express* trainset to ensure that the train is working properly.

1:53 A.M. CITY BOUND. Coach passengers prepare to embark on the double-decker Superliner that will carry passengers from Walnut Ridge, Ark., to Chicago.

2:27 A.M. (NEARLY) EMPTY STATION. It is a rare moment of quiet in New York Penn Station. In less than five hours, an army of train passengers and commuters will throng the station.

3:16 A.M. PROTECTING AMERICA'S RAILROAD. Sergeants Joseph Robbins (left) and Louis Lupinacci patrol Penn Station predawn.

3:17 A.M. DOWNTIME. Taking advantage of a moment when few trains are running, heavy-duty maintenance

3:21 A.M. STRETCHING OUT.
A passenger sleeps on the *Silver Star*, a
train that runs from New York to Miami.

4:50 A.M. AT THE CONSOLIDATED NATIONAL OPERATIONS CENTER. In Wilmington,
Del., dispatchers fill all the conductor, engineer, and crew member vacancies for assignments
on the day's trains.

The name "Amtrak" is
the blending of the words
"America" and "track."
Amtrak is also known as
the National Railroad
Passenger Corporation.

5:33 A.M. JUST BEFORE DAYBREAK. Conductor Ryan
Riddell starts his workday by walking to the train in Richmond, Va.

6:10 A.M. BAD WEATHER COMMUTE. Passengers stand in the rain as a *Northeast Regional* train slows to a stop in Ashland, Va.

6:16 A.M. COFFEE TIME. Sometimes trains run on caffeine.

7:09 A.M. THE EYE-OPENER. The chef on the *Empire Builder*, which runs from Seattle to Chicago, prepares to serve passengers a hearty morning meal.

7:18 A.M. GREENER TRAVEL. In Durham, N.C., Conductor Chrissie Wetmore helps a passenger unload a bike.

7:20 A.M. **BLUE FLAG PROTECTION.** This well-known signal, shown here in Fort Worth, Texas, tells all train and engine employees that work is being performed on the track and that it is unsafe to pass.

7:59 A.M. **END OF THE NIGHT (SHIFT).** Morning is the end of the day for *Auto Train* Engineers Ernie Alston and Sean Daughtry. Here, in Lorton, Va., they hand down a grip—railroad lingo for crew members' personal effects.

8:00 A.M. **SAFETY AT A GLANCE.** Assistant Conductor Ke'ke Touray keeps a watchful eye on the platform at New Carrollton, Md., as her train leaves the station.

8:02 A.M. REPORTING FROM HIGH PLAINS. In Rugby, N.D., Agent Duane Viach provides an update on the departure of the *Empire Builder* headed for Seattle.

8:27 A.M. A GENTLE TOUCH. Station Agent Pat Calton in Longview, Texas, loads passenger baggage onto a cart in anticipation of the arrival of the *Texas Eagle*.

8:48 A.M. IN CONTROL. In Washington Union Station, Assistant Conductor Kara Byrnes directs the movement of a 75-ton locomotive via hand signal.

8:51 A.M. CHANGING A FLAT. In Fort Worth, Texas, workers replace a set of wheels on a Superliner sleeper. Trains require constant maintenance, and the wheelsets need to be replaced every

8:55 A.M. RAIL MEETS ROAD. In several locations around the country, including here in Stockton, Calif., rail travel is supplemented by Amtrak-run bus service.

9:08 A.M. THE TEST. Machinist Harvey McCann checks the accuracy of air pressure gauges. The air pressure system is an integral part of a train's main method of braking.

9:10 A.M. FIXING IT. Mechanic Larry Taylor assembles an Amfleet coach seat in the Bear, Del., maintenance facility.

9:16 A.M. STEP RIGHT UP. In Tacoma, Wash., Conductor Jim Barry examines a ticket as a passenger mounts the yellow step box and boards an Amtrak *Cascades* train.

9:24 A.M. SMOOTHING THE WAY. Paint shop employee Eddie Purnell sands cabinet doors in a Superliner lounge car at the Beech Grove, Ind., maintenance facility.

9:29 A.M. UPDATING. Mechanic Bill Calliger moves a forklift full of new Superliner coach seats at the Beech Grove, Ind., maintenance facility.

9:45 A.M. **A GOOD START.** On a morning run to Boston, Lead Service Attendant Martina Brewbaker prepares to serve breakfast to first class passengers on the *Acela Express*.

9:57 A.M. **LIFTING IT UP.** Two massive hydraulic jacks elevate an 85-foot-long Amfleet coach at the Bear, Del., maintenance facility so that work can be performed on the undercarriage and suspension system.

10:32 A.M. **ELECTRONIC AGE.** Amtrak staffer Steve Reynolds in Chicago keeps track of the budget for station improvements in his region.

10:02 A.M. **MAKING WHAT WE NEED.** A welder fabricates protective equipment that will be installed on the underbelly of a P-42 locomotive. Amtrak technicians fabricate many key machine parts in-house.

10:33 A.M. **FEEL THE SPARK.** At Bear, Del., Electrician William Burt makes sure the automatic doors are in perfect working order before this Amfleet Business class car is put into service.

10:43 A.M. UP THE POLE. An Amtrak lineman in Rheems, Pa., inspects the wires that provide power to the trains running between Philadelphia and Harrisburg.

10:52 A.M. HANDCRAFTED. While some elements of the railroad are highly automated, Terry Shane goes old school as she posts crew assignments on a magnetic board in Seattle, Wash.

11:00 A.M. CLEAR DIRECTIONS. Kurt Laird, general superintendent Pacific Northwest Division, puts the final polish on operational guidelines that will be read and followed by several hundred railroad employees.

11:10 A.M. A SHINY PLACE TO EAT. Sheet Metal Fabricator Tyrone Harris rebuilds a dining car at the Beech Grove, Ind., maintenance facility.

Nearly

60%

of trains operate in excess of

90

miles per hour.

11:17 A.M. MOVE OVER RACHAEL RAY. At Amtrak's test kitchen in Wilmington, Del., Chef Christian Hannah creates new menu items for Amtrak passengers.

11:22 A.M. STAY SAFE. An Amtrak employee in Wilmington, Del., flashes the orange W board while train engineers blow one long and one short blast of the whistle, signaling track workers that a train is approaching.

11:42 A.M. THE WHEELS THAT RIDE THE RAILS. Machinists Glen Johnston and John Brosnan put the wheels onto the axle of an AEM-7 locomotive at the Wilmington Maintenance Facility.

11:44 A.M. LAST-MINUTE ADJUSTMENT. In Seattle, Lead Machinist Gabriel Robles replaces a valve on the braking system of a train that will soon depart for Los Angeles.

11:53 A.M. TESTING: ONE, TWO, THREE. Machinist Roy Hatten tests the brakes. Before a train leaves the station, a team of machinists makes sure the operating systems are in tip-top shape.

11:57 A.M. THE VOICE.

12:18 P.M. PRAISE

12:20 P.M. **PROVISIONS. Lead Service Attendant Vinnie Burgro stocks the lounge car on the *Sunset Limited* before it begins its 46-hour trip from New Orleans to Los Angeles.**

12:24 P.M. **KEEPING IT CLEAN. Wearing a hard hat and rubber gloves, Minerva Mejia keeps the lavatory spotless on the Washington-bound *Acela Express***

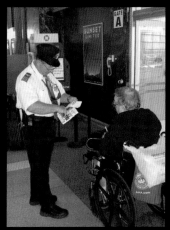

12:31 P.M.
ALL ABOARD. Conductor Curt Clement collects a ticket from a passenger boarding the westbound *Sunset Limited*.

12:35 P.M.
WHATCHA GOT COOKIN'? Dorothy Biro serves the lunchtime crowd on the eastbound *Empire Builder* that runs from Seattle to Chicago.

12:38 P.M.
RUNNING ON DIESEL. In the Northeast, passenger trains run on electricity from overhead wires. In the rest of the country, they're diesel powered. Here, a train gets refueled at Portland, Ore.

12:45 P.M.
SIGNATURE DESIGN. Every conductor has a unique ticket punch. Here, Woody Bond makes his mark on the *Piedmont*, which runs between Raleigh and Charlotte, N.C.

More facts

Amtrak operates 15 long-distance trains on a national network of routes ranging in length from 764 to 2,438 miles. These trains provide the only Amtrak service in 23 states and at nearly half of the stations served. They are also the only intercity passenger transportation service in an increasing number of communities.

Of the miles traveled by Amtrak trains, 70 percent are on tracks owned by other railroads. Known as host railroads, they range from large publicly traded companies, state and local government agencies, and small businesses. Amtrak pays them for use of their track and the resources required to operate Amtrak trains. Payments in fiscal year 2009 totaled more than $121.9 million for nearly 27 million train miles. The six largest host railroads for Amtrak trains are
- BNSF, 6.8 million train miles
- Union Pacific, 6.19 million train miles
- CSX Transportation, 5.90 million train miles
- Norfolk Southern, 2.49 million train miles
- Canadian National, 1.46 million train miles
- Metro North, 1.34 million train miles

Amtrak owns 363 miles of the 456-mile Northeast Corridor that connects Washington, Philadelphia, New York, and Boston. This is the busiest passenger line in the country, with trains regularly reaching speeds of 125-150 mph.

Over the 104 miles of Amtrak-owned track between Philadelphia and Harrisburg, the first new high-speed corridor in the 21st century, trains can travel up to 110 mph.

Amtrak is the only railroad in North America to maintain rights-of-way for service at speeds in excess of 100 mph, and its engineering forces maintain more than 350 route-miles of track for 100+ mph service.

Amtrak has 17 tunnels that consist of 29.7 miles of track and 1,186 bridges consisting of 42.5 miles of track.

Amtrak-owned equipment includes 1,518 Amfleet, Superliner, Viewliner, and other passenger cars. It also owns 459 locomotives, 80 *Auto Train* vehicle carriers, and 101 baggage cars.

In addition, it operates 140 state-owned passenger cars and 22 locomotives.

There are heavy maintenance facilities in Wilmington, Del., Bear, Del., and Beech Grove, Ind. Other maintenance facilities are located in Washington, D.C., New York City, Boston, Chicago, New Orleans, Los Angeles, Oakland, Seattle, Rensselaer, N.Y., Niagara Falls, N.Y., and Hialeah, Fla.

12:59 P.M. CALIFORNIA FLEET. With the population growth in the Golden State—and worries about auto traffic—ridership is skyrocketing. Here, a worker washes an Amtrak California train.

1:09 P.M. LEARNING THE ROPES. Ticket Agent Ghislain Daniel shows trainee Felicia Boulware how to issue a passenger ticket in Washington Union Station.

1:17 P.M. SAFETY FIRST. An onboard services crew briefing in Seattle includes Service Attendant/Train Attendant Robynn Widhalm, Lead Service Attendant Joe Cumiford, Chef Deborah Brown, Onboard Service Supervisor Maragaret Collins, Train Attendant Mary Hooper, Food Specialist Dale Villines, and Train Attendant Rodgie Woods.

1:26 P.M. BREAK DOWN LANE. Amtrak's pit crew in Chicago makes an unscheduled repair in order to keep the trains

1:42 P.M. WORKING ON THE RAILROAD. Assisted by Bryan Maffa and Edward Morrell, Signal Maintainer David Dinaro replaces the cover to a switch he has just fixed.

1:30 P.M. SNACKING THROUGH THE MIDWEST. Lead Service Attendant Ken Homko sells snacks to passengers on the *Missouri River Runner*, which runs from Kansas City to St. Louis.

1:46 P.M. SERVICE WITH A SMILE. Theresa Hammond serves a soft drink to a thirsty passenger on a New York-bound *Acela Express*.

1:48 P.M. BUILDING A WORK-FORCE. Human Resources expert Christina Arenas ensures that the company hires a diverse and talented workforce.

2:09 P.M. **COUNTING THE CASH.** Seattle Ticket Agent Kara Andrew reconciles the proceeds of the day's ticket sales.

1:59 P.M. **TEAMWORK. Conductor Jeff Busold and Assistant Conductor Paula Turner choreograph their moves to smooth the departure of this *Empire Service* train at Yonkers, N.Y.**

2:10 P.M. **START OF THE SHIFT.** Three members of the westbound *Empire Builder* crew, Jeremy Jacobson, Starr Ivey, and Annette Spencer, prepare to board their train in Chicago and begin their two-day journey to Seattle.

2:14 P.M. **ROOM WITH A VIEW.** Welder Dennis McGinness adds windows to an old café car to convert it into a new passenger coach at the Bear, Del,, maintenance facility.

2:27 P.M. SWEET DREAMS. Sleeping Car Attendant Manuel Walton prepares an upper berth. The moment a room is empty, attendants get it ready for the next passenger.

2:30 P.M. PARKING THE TRAIN. After passengers disembark, Engineer Mark Rowland prepares to leave his empty train in the yard at St. Louis.

2:40 P.M. IF IT'S BROKE, WE FIX IT. Bear, Del., Welder Marcelus Bethea puts a suspension system back together.

2:46 P.M. SCENIC SKYLINE. A passenger takes in the view aboard the New York-bound *Acela*.

3:08 P.M. AFTER THE

3:09 P.M. IT COMES FROM THE TOP. President and CEO Joe Boardman, the ninth president of Amtrak, keeps an eye on all aspects of the system.

3:25 P.M. EVERYTHING IN ITS PLACE. Kenny Carter helps keep spare train parts organized in the Material Control warehouse in New Orleans.

3:31 P.M. PRACTICE MAKES PERFECT. Trainee Sharon Rich learns to operate a high-speed train on the *Acela* simulator at the Wilmington Training Center as instructor Jay Gilfillan looks on.

The name "Acela" was created by combining the words "acceleration" and "excellence." *Acela Express* trains can attain speeds of 150 mph.

3:32 P.M. SAFE TRAVELS. Road Foreman Norma Jean Kirby checks the speed of the northbound *Vermonter*.

3:45 P.M. **ATTENTION TO DETAIL.** Joe Wenclawiak makes sure every date and time listed on the public timetables are correct.

4:05 P.M. **ON ALERT.** Sergeant Gabriel Bernson and his partner Niki patrol the train.

4:17 P.M. **THE BIG GULP.** John Madden provides the *Coast Starlight* with fresh water in Portland, Ore.

4:25 P.M. **MAKING A CONNECTION.** Roxanne Williams provides travel information in Washington Union Station.

4:35 P.M. **STRIKE A POSE.** A Marketing team from headquarters takes a beauty shot of Amtrak's pride and joy while on an official photo shoot.

4:37 P.M. **MAY I HELP YOU?** The Mid-Atlantic Reservation Sales Contact Center outside of Philadelphia, Pa., handles thousands of passenger inquiries a day.

4:38 P.M. **WINE-TASTING COUNTRY.** Service Attendant Alan Schechter pours a fine vintage for a passenger in the Pacific Parlour (first class lounge) Car on the Seattle-to-Los Angeles *Coast Starlight*.

4:54 P.M. ALL ABOARD. A Boston-bound *Acela Express* prepares to leave Washington, D.C., loaded with business executives who have completed their day's work in the nation's capitol.

4:57 P.M. MOBILE OFFICE. A busy executive extends his workday en route to the train.

4:59 P.M. A NOSE FOR TROUBLE. Amtrak Police K-9 Ivan intently searches a bag.

5:00 P.M. FRESH PRODUCE. Chef Kenneth Lahr prepares salad for passengers on the San Antonio-bound *Texas Eagle*.

5:09 P.M. C'MON BACK. Conductor Woody Bond keeps his hand on the train's emergency brake as the train reverses into the station at Charlotte, N.C.

5:37 P.M. **TALENT BANK.** Veteran Road Foreman Harry Hibbert hands Human Resource whiz Nicole Donnelly the resume of a potential new employee.

5:45 P.M. **A MAGICAL JOURNEY.** A young passenger experiences the wonders of train travel for the first time.

5:46 P.M. **NOT THE CORPORATE LADDER.** Engineer Matt Reinert clambers back into his office after inspecting his train en route to New York.

6:52 P.M. **GOLDEN YEARS.** A well-traveled couple savors the scenery from the eastbound *Empire Builder*.

6:57 P.M. **HANDLING WITH CARE.** Conductor Anthony C. Milazzo prepares to unload baggage in Orlando, Fla.

7:25 P.M. **FAMILY PORTRAIT. Passengers pose in front of the *Southwest Chief* in La Junta, Colo.**

7:54 P.M. **READY TO GO. Conductor Andrea Olson waits for the okay, so she can tell the engineer to move the train out of Chicago Union Station.**

7:55 P.M. **LEARNING THE ROPES. In Chicago, Stationmaster Angela Breninger instructs trainee Keenan Lett on the finer points of running a major transportation hub.**

8:16 P.M. INTO THE NIGHT. After a brief stop in Greenwood, Miss., the northbound *City of New Orleans* speeds on its way.

8:22 P.M. FRONT LINE SERVICE. Ticket Agent Heidi Munkres in Bellingham, Wash., checks on a request from a customer.

8:50 P.M. MAKING MEMORIES. After a soothing late-night ride, a family prepares to disembark in Savannah, Ga.

9:36 P.M. A WATCHFUL EYE. From his vantage point atop a seven-story tower in Chicago, Yardmaster Vashon L. Edmondson Sr. surveys his domain.

10:12 P.M. QUALITY TIME. As the northbound *Silver Meteor* rolls through Georgia on its way to New York, a family plays cards.

11:52 P.M. ON TIME. Even in the midnight hour, Conductor Susan Poleto and Assistant Conductor Mark Fremgen keep their *Empire Service* train running on schedule at the Poughkeepsie, N.Y., station.

IN MEMORIAM

In recognition and tribute to Amtrak employees who lost their lives
in the performance of their duties.

Donna M. Adams

Diego M. Almarez

Caesar F. Arguelles

Mitchell Bates

Henry R. Brooks, Jr.

Forest A. Burke

Marvin L. Burton

Denis Callahan

Robert Charles, Jr.

Albert S. Chinchar

William F. Clark

Robert S. Collins

Howard L. Colton

Henry L. Cooper

Charles Crawford

Joseph D. Dean

James R. Dutton, Sr.

R. Easter

Larry W. Edenfield

John R. Elliot

James G. Evans

Jerome E. Evans

Michael Eyerly

John Fabe

Scott Fletcher

Ronald Gallagher

Richard E. George

Albert S. Giudice

Eugene T. Goulet

Dennis Griffin

Billy R. Hall

David Hopper

Richard Hutchison

Robert A. Isacs

Daniel C. Jenovese

John M. Jensen

Wayne A. King

Aaron C. King, Jr.

Jerome H. Knoble

Paul G. Landers

Glenn A. Loveless

Edward E. McMillon

Brian Moroska

Arthur J. Moses

Randall L. Moses

Kevin M. Murphy

Thomas M. Ormiston

Michael G. Passarella

T. Pershing

Kenneth D. Plouffe

Ronald W. Quaintance

Donald J. Rafferty

Davis E. Rambo

Nicholas Riccardi

Ernest L. Russ

Richard Russo

Steven Rychwalski

Teague R. Sligh

Michael Soldan

David Sproul

William C. Strohmaier

James H. Suggs

Peter L. Sylvester

Michael L. Taggert

John B. Thomas

Neville B. Thomas, Jr.

Michael D. Vinet

Elmer Vogel

Peter Wells

Donald P. Williams

John Wilson

Robert Brooks Woodward

Joseph Zoch

— ACKNOWLEDGMENTS —

THE GENESIS OF THIS BOOK was a casual conversation in Joe McHugh's office sometime in late 2008 during the preparation for the Washington Union Station centennial celebration. Joe, always filled with wonderful ideas, mused that it would be great to have a table-top book celebrating a day in the life of Amtrak to commemorate our 40th anniversary as America's Railroad. Some 18 months later, this project, a real labor of love, began in earnest. The team was assembled and quickly jelled. Most of us already worked together in some capacity. Some of us had long histories and worked for the railroad for close to 30 years. Others were relatively new to this corporation. We have mutual respect for one another, we enjoy working together, and we all wanted this project to succeed.

We had the good fortune of bringing Peg Tyre on board as editorial director. Peg provided discipline, her great talent, refereeing skills, and a necessary sense of humor. We are deeply indebted to her. Thanks also to Mark Thompson and Randy Rehberg from Kalmbach Books, who patiently guided us through this journey, and Tom Ford at Kalmbach for design.

And we wanted to convey our thanks to the states and communities that have supported us, to the railfan groups who both champion our cause and challenge us to strive to do continually better, and to the traveling public without whom we would not be America's Railroad. We wanted to create a book that would tell our story and who better to do that than our own employees, past and present. We are hopeful that we have told our tale in our own unique voice.

There are many excellent photographers among Amtrak's employees, and they were selected to go to various parts of our railroad network and take pictures for us. Others submitted photos from their collections. We appreciate all they contributed. You will see their photo credits throughout the book. Bruce Goldberg, Ann Owens, and Brian Roman provided a wealth of historic promotional materials. Collin King performed magic with photo enhancements.

Ann also took the lead on the Day in the Life section, maintained scrupulous files, and has endless energy and historic knowledge of our archival photo collection.

Matt Donnelly, Steve Ostrowski, and Doug Riddell contributed photos, traveled to capture just the right images, and are true partners in this endeavor.

Rob Ripperger wrote some of the magnificent prose contained between these covers and provided some statistics, and we shared the timeline research task.

Josh Raymond contacted past company leaders and guided them in their chapter introductions. With great finesse, he was able to get a myriad of our former executives to respond by deadline, and he artfully edited their pieces.

Chris Jagodzinski and Marc Magliari graciously contributed their time and knowledge of the railroad in order to assist with caption writing.

Matt also took on the role of photo editor and lead caption writer. The magnitude of this task seemed to grow exponentially with each passing week.

The skills of Nan Fredman, Patrick Kidd, and Margaret Sherry are also reflected in these pages.

On behalf of the book team, I would like to express our gratitude to our various supervisors, who gave us the green light to work on this book in addition to our regularly assigned duties and who understand our passion for excellence.

Most importantly, deep appreciation goes to Joe McHugh, who supported this endeavor with his usual intelligence, masterful editing and writing skills, humor, and faith in the team. Everyone should be privileged enough to work for such a gentleman at one time in his or her life.

Lastly, we want to give a big thank-you to our respective spouses, partners, children, and pets for putting up with the late nights and occasional bad moods.

I am so lucky to work with such incredible people whom I now call my friends. This was an experience I will always treasure.

Suzi Andiman
Editor, www.GreatAmericanStations.com

Roger Lewis, 1971-1974

Paul Reistrup, 1974-1978

Alan S. Boyd, 1978-1982

W. Graham Claytor Jr., 1982-1993

Thomas Downs, 1993-1998

George Warrington, 1998-2002

David Gunn, 2002-2005

Alex Kummant, 2006-2008

Joe Boardman, 2008-present